Contents

INDEX ON CENSORSHIP

VOLUME 45 NUMBER 01

SPRING 2016

EDITOR
Rachael Jolley
DEPUTY EDITOR
Vicky Baker
SUB EDITORS
Sean Anderson, Charlotte Bailey, Alex
Dudok de Wit, Jan Fox, Sally Gimson

CONTRIBUTING EDITORS
Kaya Genç (Turkey), Natasha Joseph
(South Africa), Jemimah Steinfeld,
Irene Caselli (Argentina)

EDITORIAL ASSISTANT
Josie Timms
DESIGN
Matthew Hasteley
COVER
Ben Jennings
THANKS TO:
Jodie Ginsberg, Sean Gallagher,
Ryan McChrystal

Magazine printed by Page Bros.,
Norwich, UK

Index on Censorship, 92-94 Tooley Street, London SE1 2TH, United Kingdom
+44 (0) 207 260 2660, www.indexoncensorship.org

Sneaky Shakespeare smuggles in protest

EDITORIAL

45(01): 3/5 | DOI: 10.1177/0306422016642998

by **Rachael Jolley**

THEATRE, IN WHATEVER form it takes, tells us something about society. Sometimes the stories are uncomfortable, but they need to be explored.

Telling stories that challenge societal realities requires performers to negotiate their way around obstacles. In authoritarian countries with heavy censorship, performing works of "established" or "historic" playwrights can give actors the chance to tackle significant themes that would otherwise never be allowed.

Poet Robert Frost said writing free verse was like playing tennis with the net down. But where nets are still up, performances of Chekhov, Shakespeare and Cicero may squeeze over a few shots, where a new and unknown writer's work would face far more rigorous opposition from the authorities. On the occasion of the 400th anniversary of Shakespeare's death, in this issue we take a look at the words of the son of Stratford and why they are still performed around the world.

One of theatre's challenges is that it must continue to make sense to all audiences, the young, the old and everyone in between. Shakespeare's plays can be ballsy, straightforward and about the ordinary. This is no doubt why his words have had influence for so long, while other playwrights have been forgotten.

This appeal, and relevance, remains a challenge for writers and directors. After university, I worked for a few months in the legendary Hull Truck theatre in the northeast of England, led by artistic director and playwright John Godber. What Godber did in a working-class city where few people would think, "Hey, let's go see a play tonight", was to write and stage plays that sounded like they were about normal people and normal things.

The most famous, Bouncers, is about the people who do door security in nightclubs. A tale of ordinary life, it was funny, and lots of people came to see it in the little theatre in the untarted-up bit of Hull, around the corner from where millions of milk floats loaded up. And people who didn't normally go to the theatre thought it was alright for them and told their families and their friends it was a laugh, and so more and more of them came to see more Godber plays. I re-read Bouncers a month ago, and I realised (I guess, I had forgotten), it was more than just funny. There's real stuff in there about how people live and what they dream, and how they find a compromise with life, and what needs to change. Hard stuff. Important stuff. Social comment. Hidden in there among the jokes.

That's how theatre informs us of lives beyond our own. And that's why, sometimes, governments fear it. And that's why in another place, and under another type of government, a play like Bouncers might slip its social messages by those hard-line censors who might not think it's about anything but some fat bald guys who work on the →

→ door at a dodgy nightclub having a chat.

But the other role of stories, plays and art is that they also have the power to goad, protest and say stuff that normally can't be said. Sometimes stories make what had been outrageous or out-of-the-ordinary feel more acceptable. Sometimes fiction can go places where newspapers can't, but still deal with the real.

That's how theatre informs us of lives beyond our own. And that's why, sometimes, governments fear it

Arthur Miller's 1952 play The Crucible used the Salem Witch Trials to take a poke at the power of accusation and public panic happening in McCarthyite trials. During this period in the USA, people from postmen to Hollywood producers were called to give evidence to the House of Un-American Activities Committee, which aimed to "out" those with left wing or pro-Communist views as dangerous, leaving thousands of people blacklisted and unemployed. Despite the horrifically charged climate of the "reds under the bed" era, which meant former stars such as Charlie Chaplin and Orson Welles were forced into exile, Miller was still able to get his play produced. It remains a classic, still relevant after all these years.

The similarities between Salem and the McCarthy trials were obvious to those that thought about it. Sometimes those who are appointed as censors are not the thinking types. So ideas slip by them. And that can be useful.

Shakespeare, of course, has plenty of controversy, inspiration and power within his plays. It's just less obvious to those who aren't paying attention. There's nothing mousy and out-of-date about the speech of roaring rhetoric of Henry V to his rag-taggle followers, to raise spirits and to go forth against a much larger army: "We few, we happy few, we band of brothers, for he today that sheds his blood with me shall be my brother."

Henry V's speech could still be used to rally the troops. They still feel pointed, and relevant. Yet because Shakespeare is Shakespeare, his words and ideas escape the red pen of the brutal censor more than others do. "Centuries out of date", the censors and government red-penners must think. "Can't do any harm."

So in some countries, Zimbabwe among them, Shakespeare is used to smuggle ideas of protest past those who veto that kind of thing. Playwright Elizabeth Zaza Muchemwa says in her country where there are so many restrictions on theatre companies (page 22), Shakespeare appears to slip through the net, raising storylines of senility of a king (King Lear) and of overthrowing of a leader (Julius Caesar), which feel important to Zimbabwean citizens dealing with the long last days of an elderly ruler. Shakespeare's writing continues to inspire, she says.

But the badge of Shakespeare doesn't always mean productions will escape the long reach of the law. In 1981, a Turkish production of A Midsummer Night's Dream came to the stage as a military government stepped up its power. As Index's Turkey editor Kaya Genç outlines (page 48) any public event, newspaper article, poem or artistic production carrying even the slightest trace of dissent against the military authority was certain to be punished. This production was felt to have highlighted the relationship between the elite and the rest (the rude mechanicals) and how status was used for power. Eight members of the cast ended up shaven-headed in prison in the next few months. The play did not squeeze by. It was noticed.

Leading Turkish theatre director Kemal Aydoğan, who produced the latest version of the play in Turkey, tells Index that the

LEFT: The madness of
King Lear. Wu Hsing-
kuo in the eponymous
play in Edinburgh,
Scotland, 2011

Dream has a strong relevance to troubles in his nation today. He sees a parallel between the struggle between desire and the law, and the dream of the forest, a place where desire and equality dominates.

Also see Jan Fox's umissable, long-form essay exploring the love/hate relationship the USA has, and has had, with Shakespeare (page 12). The Puritan founders felt all theatre was beyond the pale, and looked frowningly on its ribaldry. So this is a nation with a core of censorship at odds with its commitment to its First Amendment freedom of expression. LA-based Fox covers why Shakespeare still upsets parents because of its drama around everything from teenage suicide to under-age sex. "Shakespeare is telling us about our secret self and that's what people are aware of," believes Gail Kern Paster, editor of the US-based journal Shakespeare Quarterly.

While plays by established writers can smuggle through dissent and protest in countries where strict rules of performance exist, as nations move towards greater democracy then the public must expect and demand far more provocative, outrageous and openly challenging material from its theatre as well as welcoming the established masterpieces. We should all look forward to the signs of those times. ⊗

Rachael Jolley is editor of Index on Censorship. She tweets @londoninsider

SPECIAL REPORT

Staging Shakespearean dissent:
plays that protest, provoke and slip by the censors

MAIN: Inside Shakespeare's Globe theatre in London

Credit: See-Li / Alamy

Rising star

45(01): 8/11 | DOI: 10.1177/0306422016642999

China has swung from banning Shakespeare to embracing his work. Why is the Bard so in favour, asks **Jemimah Steinfeld**

REFERRED TO AS Shashibiya or Old Man Sha, Shakespeare's star is shining bright this year in China. On top of a UK government-funded initiative to translate his complete works into Mandarin, the Royal Shakespeare Company has embarked on its first major tour of China. Called King and Country, the tour includes performances of Henry IV Part I, Henry IV Part II and Henry V in Beijing, Shanghai and Hong Kong.

None of this would have been possible 40 years ago, when China was still under the dark shadow of the Cultural Revolution, between 1966 and 1976. Shakespeare was banned, alongside a series of other Western playwrights, his work was labelled bourgeois and lumped into the doomed category of moral and spiritual pollution. When the government finally lifted their ban on Shakespeare in 1977, it was seen as a sign of political liberalisation. Indeed his coming back into favour was evidence that the Cultural Revolution really was over and that China had moved on.

But Shakespeare's re-emergence was still political, albeit of a different political nature. After the death of communist leader Mao Zedong in the late 1970s, a new ideology was being propagated. This ideology supported a market economy under the banner of socialism with Chinese characteristics. Shakespeare could easily adapt to this new look – and his plays quickly did. Enter the era of the big and brash Shakespeare shows,

which continue today. State productions are typically extravagant and driven by a message: China is modern, culturally plural and open to the West.

Chinese-British actor Daniel York was part of one of these big productions. He acted in a 2006 bilingual version of King Lear in Shanghai, the bare bones of which he outlined to Index. It was set in a future Shanghai, which is a leading international centre with a bilingual population, where King Lear was played by a Hong Kong billionaire businessman. The play climaxed with a battle, as in the original, only the location had shifted away from the jagged cliffs of Dover to the heat of the Chinese stock exchange.

Whatever the political mood, the Chinese government uses Shakespeare to reflect it. It's made easy by how Shakespeare is taught in China, namely in the Chinese department as part of world literature, and the drama department, but not in the English department. Tuition is in Mandarin and so the pupil is directly at the mercy of the teacher.

As scholar Murray Levith writes of Shakespeare: "Perhaps more than any other nation, China has used a great artist to forward its own ideology rather than meet him on his own ground."

The Chinese Communist Party does not have a monopoly on Shakespeare and what ideologies are advanced through his plays. Other Chinese voices have come to the fore,

Credit: Shanghai Shakespeare

some of which are overtly critical of the government. A case in point is the film, Prince of the Himalayas. This 2009 movie, based on Hamlet, was an instant hit, airing at cinemas across the country and even spawning stage recreations. The film – shot in Tibet – was about a prince who returns to his kingdom to find he has been usurped. The allegory of modern Tibet was not lost on many movie goers. Yet it was set in a pre-modern mythical kingdom and it was Shakespeare, so it was allowed. In some instances Shakespeare can extend the limits of free speech.

Other interpretations are less political and yet still use Shakespeare as a means of furthering their own agenda. Alexa Huang, an expert on Shakespeare in China, told Index about watching The Taming of the Shrew in Beijing back in 2006.

"They took the taming literally, disciplining Katherine for her behaviour," said Huang, who is a professor at George Washington University. She's also seen productions of King Lear, which have been interpreted in China as an allegory for fulfilling filial duty. Unlike the typically sympathetic portrayal of Cordelia, in China she is seen as stepping out of line, a defiant character who publically shames her father. Placed within the context of a country which has a long way to go in terms of female liberation and still values Confucianism, the message behind both of these examples is clear.

"With Shakespeare you almost have a total free licence," said Huang. That certainly might be the case. China's current president, Xi Jinping, is a huge fan of Shakespeare. He even went out of his way to seek banned copies of the plays during the Cultural Revolution.

Alison Friedman from Ping Pong Productions, a company that seeks to bring China and the world closer through the arts, has a similar view. She helped stage a US version of A Midsummer Night's Dream in 2014. Friedman said she has had no problems producing her work in China.

"Generally speaking (and it certainly →

ABOVE: Actors Du Gang, Vivi Zhang and Barbara Zheng during a scene from Shanghai Shakespeare's production of Pericles. The play contains scenes that were banished from the stage for more than two centuries as they were deemed vulgar and offensive

9

INDEXONCENSORSHIP.ORG

ABOVE: Members of the Shanghai Peking Opera Troupe perform the play La Venganza del Principe Zi Dan (The Revenge of the Prince Zi Dan), based on Hamlet, during the 40th International Cervantino Festival at the Juárez Theatre in Guanajuato, Mexico, in 2012

→ changes when the pendulum swings, which it does), we find if you don't bother them they don't bother you."

She added: "When it comes to the performing arts, China is a much more open space than the outside world thinks it is. What a lot of young and independent artists face is lack of funding rather than political persecution."

Naturally part of the success of more controversial Shakespeare interpretations lies in the main arena being the stage. The CCP does not approach theatre in quite the way they do other more mainstream media.

"Playwrights joke that censors only pay attention to films and TV. They [the censors] are busy. They don't read between the lines and they're not literary critics," said Huang.

This does not mean that anything goes. Huang highlights another play, based on Hamlet, which has yet to see the light of day. Called Tomorrow We Are Carrying The Coffin To The Cemetery, it was written by a young playwright straight after the Tiananmen Square massacre in 1989. He never allowed it to be performed because of fear of death threats.

And back to the futuristic Shanghai of King Lear, York believes self-censorship came into play. "It steered clear of politics, corruption and triads," he said.

Shakespeare's introduction into China can be traced back to British colonial efforts in the 19th century, and a translation of Charles and Mary Lamb's Tales From Shakespeare (1807), was published in 1903 and 1904, with the first complete translation of a Shakespeare play appearing in 1921 when Hamlet was published.

Performances of Shakespeare's plays did not gain their audiences in China just against a backdrop of the political. Rather, they were

translation came from the Soviet Union, having been reworked to reflect Marxist-Leninist values. King Lear was described as "a portrayal of the shaken economic foundations of feudal society"; Romeo and Juliet was about "the desire of the bourgeoisie to shake off the yoke of the feudal code of ethics". Then there was Hamlet, the most translated of Shakespeare's plays and the most in line with the CCP. Bian Zhilin's 50,000-word essay on Hamlet from 1957 set the tone. Bian depicts Hamlet as someone who aligns himself with society's underdogs.

"Through his bitter thinking (ie his soliloquies) and his mad words, Hamlet realises

China's president, Xi Jinping, is a huge fan of Shakespeare, and even went out of his way to seek banned copies of the plays during the Cultural Revolution

always central to the political scene. They grew in popularity in line with a new form of theatre. *Huaja*, known as spoken drama, was more confrontational in nature. It was in direct contrast to *xiqu*, Chinese opera, which dominated the stage until the early 20th century. China's young revolutionaries and reformers viewed *xiqu* as decorative. *Huaja*, by contrast, could serve a political or educational purpose.

An early 20th-century performance of The Merchant of Venice exemplifies this. Influenced by ideas of female liberation coming out of the new women's movements, students at Shanghai's St John's University staged the play with the character of Portia given a very positive portrayal.

As the political mood shifted in China in the middle of the century, so too did the interpretation of Shakespeare. Under the early communists, the bulk of literature in

the social inequality and the suffering that the masses have borne. Such an experience not only makes Hamlet hate his enemies more but also gives him more strength to carry on his fight."

"This was Shakespeare with Chinese socialist characteristics," said Huang. "The belief was that Shakespeare spoke for the proletariat."

China might have largely moved on from thinking Shakespeare speaks for the proletariat, or even that Shakespeare is Western spiritual pollution, but utilising Shakespeare for a political or social cause continues. Time will tell how he will be used in the future. ⊗

Jemimah Steinfeld is a contributing editor for Index. She previously reported for CNN from Beijing, China. Her book Little Emperors and Material Girls in Modern China (I.B. Taurus) is out now

When the show doesn't go on ...

45(01): 12/17 | DOI: 10.1177/0306422016643000

From a lesbian kiss in As You Like It to a Malcolm X-styled Tybalt, new interpretations of Shakespeare's plays continue to cause controversy in the USA. **Jan Fox** reports on productions that were shut down, and the students who dare to challenge conventions

WHEN THE PILGRIM Fathers arrived in the American colonies, theatre was a dirty word. Puritan thinking forbade such abomination. While Shakespeare's written work garnered respect from Americans over the years, public performance often remained contentious and still does to this day.

"The plays were safe in themselves – the subversion would come through performance choices to convey subversive messages," said Gail Kern Paster, director emerita of the Folger Shakespeare Library in Washington DC and editor of Shakespeare Quarterly, a scholarly journal devoted to Shakespeare.

"It's one thing to read about a black moor [Othello] killing his white wife but another thing to see it on stage – it was considered appalling in 19th-century America. The role of Othello couldn't be performed by a black actor until after World War II. So Paul Robeson could play the role in London, but not in the USA.

"Drama is potentially a dangerous instrument. Shakespeare is telling us about our secret self and that's what people are afraid of.

"In a way we can step back from the idea of censorship and look at it as social expression and the way the plays challenged us then, now and will do forever. Theatres put ideas out into the world and don't tell you what to do with them but make you think – which can upset the authorities."

Sometimes, said Paster, the upset comes from the audience itself. A production of As You Like It at Folger Theatre cast a female actor in the role of Touchstone. In the play, Touchstone falls for Audrey the Goat Girl and they kiss. At an audience question-and-answer session with the cast afterwards, a girl stood up and said the kiss had made her uncomfortable.

"It was really a teaching moment because theatre is not supposed to just comfort you but also to challenge you," said Paster. "Let's think about why it's something you don't want to see. Who's allowed to fall in love with whom? Anybody can fall in love with anybody. Yes, some parents and schools and audiences get very upset but that's the function of Shakespeare's plays – to make us think as well as to entertain us."

Dramatic representation can be more than dangerous. It can be potentially deadly, said Paster.

Shakespeare contemporary Christopher Marlowe's Tamburlaine was staged in New

Some parents and schools and audiences get very upset but that's the function of Shakespeare's plays – to make us think as well as to entertain us

York by the Theatre for a New Audience at Brooklyn's Polonsky Shakespeare Center in the autumn of 2014 with black actor John Douglas Thompson in the title role. In the play Tamburlaine burns a copy of the Koran on stage.

"Of course, this was considered to be subversive, dangerous and provocative even when it was first performed in London in 1587 and just as much so now," said Paster.

"Marlowe was actually writing about

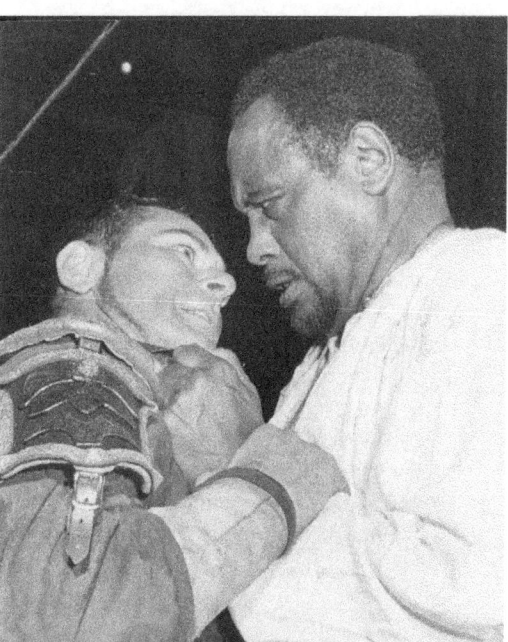

OPPOSITE: Actors Clay Westman, Bree Ogaldez and Jakeim Hart play Romeo, Juliet and Paris respectively, in a performance of Romeo and Juliet, at the Muhlenberg College in Pennsylvania

LEFT: Actors Paul Robeson and Sam Wanamaker in a Broadway production of Othello in 1943. Robeson was the first African-American to appear with a white supporting cast in a US theatre

→ atheism, not Islam. We had the scholar advisory council there and I suggested we needed to get out ahead of it and start a dialogue with the local Muslim community, which we did and there were no protests when it was performed. [The play's run was actually extended.]

Drama is potentially a dangerous instrument. Shakespeare is telling us about our secret self and that's what people are afraid of

"But it is dangerous. We are in a cultural moment where this sort of thing can get you killed. Just because it's a fictional representation, it doesn't mean you're protected – you've only got to think of those dead cartoonists at Charlie Hebdo to know that.

"Like Marlowe's, many of Shakespeare's plays push our cultural buttons – think of Shylock's lines – 'Hath not a Jew eyes' … 'Do we not revenge?'"

Sherri Young, director of the San Francisco-based African-American Shakespeare Company, understands why the plays can be contentious. "We staged Romeo and Juliet and wanted to attract a younger audience, so we cast 14 and 15 year olds. It was risky because of the sexuality and the reference to teen suicide but we talked about the process with the actors and their parents and it was a wonderful experience.

"It makes the adults nervous but the fact is that teens are being sexualised at a very young age these days, and there is a problem with teen suicide. So, while I can understand why some communities have banned Romeo and Juliet, I think that's what is dangerous – a lot of kids think they are alone and don't talk about these things and it's perhaps

‖‖

When the Capulets go to Ferguson

When a Pennsylvania college decided to use Romeo and Juliet to explore attitudes to race and gun violence, audiences reacted in an unexpected way

Romeo the bad boy? Surely that role belongs to the hot-headed Tybalt who slays Romeo's friend Mercutio and sets in motion a fatal chain of events for the star-crossed lovers?
Not in the production mounted in spring 2015 at Muhlenberg College in Allentown, Pennsylvania, where audiences were distinctly uncomfortable about love-lorn Romeo's actions.

Troy Dwyer, director and associate professor at Muhlenberg, said: "We had already started (as an ensemble) devising around the Black Lives Matter issue and thought we could amplify our message by moving into Shakespeare terrain."

"Students were interested in staging a production that would go beyond preaching to the converted in the community. We wanted to penetrate mainstream culture and it worked with Romeo and Juliet. It was a hot ticket and we were able to spark some conversations!"

Dwyer said: "We looked at Tybalt's character and his relationship with Lady Capulet (our actress was black). She saw something in Tybalt beyond the brash young man. She had a kind of maternal feeling for him, saw the softness in him."

"We started to bring in how young black men are perceived outside circles of colour and spinning the idea of what if Tybalt was a figure like Michael Brown or Tamir Rice? Both have had multi-characterisations after their deaths in the media – inside and outside the community, through family eyes and so on."

"The Capulet enclave was not dissimilar to Ferguson or our community of Allentown. The Montagues were the dominant (white) culture.

better to open the conversation."

Their productions are also a platform for environmental issues – they set The Tempest on an island of trash, a makeshift stage of garbage and plastic.

Young founded the company in 1994 to give African-American actors the opportunity to be "part of the conversation" about Shakespeare which she felt they been excluded from. Not everyone thought it was such a good idea, with opposition coming from both the black and white communities.

"I got some messages from the African-American community in the beginning, very upset and saying we needed to be doing the work of black, not white, playwrights, but as performers we should be able to do whatever we want to. We had mail from the white community in the Bay Area who were frightened as well – someone actually came up to us and said: 'You do know that Shakespeare's not black?'

"Shakespeare is always challenging our attitudes and beliefs – it really makes you think about the nature of the human condition, and you gain new insights all the time – I sometimes root for Richard III now!"

Much of the censoring of Shakespeare and other plays comes from school boards, and in an arena where student actors and young community audiences are the future professional performers and patrons of theatre. This is a concern for many.

Sarah Hoffman, youth free expression manager at the National Coalition Against Censorship, said their tool kit for schools – The Show Must Go On – is one of their most downloaded items.

"We launched it in 2014 to provide students with the resources to navigate tensions in their schools and communities and lead the fight for artistic freedom," said Hoffman.

Although there are no known cases so far of it being used to fight Shakespeare →

||||||||||||||||||||||||||||||||||||||||||||||||||||||||||||||||||||||||||||||||||||||||||||||||||||||||||||||||||||||||||||||

Joshua Harker played Tybalt as a young man who follows the nation of Islam – so we had the image of a Muslim/Malcolm X figure as Tybalt, buttoned up, in a suit."

"Romeo's killing of Tybalt is a crime of passion and partly self-defence but in our production he was driven in part by a culture that cast a lot of suspicion on Tybalt's physical body."

Audience reactions were somewhat surprising, said Dwyer. "We had good and careful feedback. Not so much from communities of colour in Allentown but primarily white folks who asked about Romeo's nature because, as Tybalt becomes more sympathetic as a character, Romeo becomes less so. This meant that upon Tybalt's death, some white audience members recoiled from Romeo's reaction. They started asking questions about his behaviour but the interesting thing was we didn't really change anything about Romeo's portrayal. We came to the conclusion that it was the world we put him in which made the audience feel his reaction was unexpected – he also

carried a gun instead of a rapier."

"We had a heavy police presence on stage (as The Prince's guard) and cast some actors of colour as police. When Romeo pulled the trigger he was executing a series of actions based on things he saw around him every day.

"We put a 'pea under the mattress' and hopefully engaged more people in the conversation. Afterwards people came up and told me it was really thought-provoking."

Dwyer readily acknowledges that Shakespeare can often slip through the censorship net where other plays might be challenged or even banned.

"I came to Shakespeare because I was interested in political statement through performance – art as protest. Shakespeare is the paragon of the Western dramatic literary canon and I learned quickly that there was a kind of cultural capital in his plays and that members of the community were more likely to turn up for a piece of Shakespeare than to pieces that were overtly political or that smelled of protest." **JF**

→ censorship specifically, students have won other battles.

"At Cherokee Trails High School in Colorado a student-written production, Evolution, about the evolution of love, included a kiss between two students of the same gender and a monologue about transsexuality. An administrator felt the topics were 'uncomfortable' and that the community was

I do think the desire to control the conversation in schools and colleges will get worse before it gets better

not ready to confront them. After the students spoke out, the administration changed course and allowed the play to go on," said Hoffman.

A production of Monty Python-inspired musical Spamalot at South Williamsport Junior-Senior High School in Pennsylvania,

was not so lucky. In 2014 the production was cancelled after the principal expressed concerns about homosexual themes. The play was not reinstated.

Hoffman said there seemed to be no pattern of which states censored the most: "Attempts at censorship happen everywhere, and over many different topics – sex, lesbian, gay, bisexual and transgender themes, offensive language, violence, religious viewpoints. Though we see many challenges from states like North Carolina, Texas and Florida, we can't assume that the most objections happen there.

"It may just be that they are most frequently reported there. There are even challenges in more liberal states like California, New York and New Jersey"

The sheer amount of censorship, especially in schools, is something that startled Howard Sherman, director of the arts integrity initiative at the drama department at The New School in New York, who became a full-time theatre advocate after being bombarded with calls for advice.

"I wasn't surprised that there was censorship – but I was surprised at the wide range of why people censor things, where the impulse comes from and the ways in which censorship is threatening," he said.

"One teacher told me she couldn't do A Midsummer Night's Dream because it's too sexual. Romeo and Juliet has also caused problems but do you shy away from it, or use it as a platform to open up more discussion and contextualise it?

"Of course there is a desire by students to do shows like Rent that may be challenged, but is a play as gentle as Almost Maine being challenged? Is this the slippery slope? One school banned a production of [1950s musical comedy] Once Upon a Mattress – I have no idea why – perhaps the word mattress alluded to bed?

"The question is, whether to fight or not? I feel it's better to get the work out there and face scrutiny rather than allow it to be

Banned Books Week

The American Library Association's Office for Intellectual Freedom promotes awareness of challenges to library materials and celebrates freedom of speech during Banned Books Week, which this year runs from 25 September to 1 October. It offers a series of events including virtual read-outs of controversial plays in local libraries and bookshops, which are broadcast on a dedicated YouTube channel. Readers around the world can join in. As part of a previous Banned Books week, the Brooklyn Book Festival did readings of Twelfth Night, The Merchant of Venice, and Romeo and Juliet.

LEFT: A scene from a production of Romeo and Juliet, directed by Troy Dwyer at the Muhlenberg College in Allentown, Pennsylvania

silenced or altered just to make it palatable – aside from recognising that teenagers are a lot smarter than many teachers and educators acknowledge. It's important. If we are only teaching that theatre is bland entertainment and not recognising its value for students, then you are saying we can always alter the world to make it a blander, safer, duller place.

"The broader question is that if there is no push back against the censors, the message is that censorship works and that's very dangerous beyond the world of entertainment.

"I do think the desire to control the conversation in schools and colleges will get worse before it gets better. We are a decade or two away from the schools being run by the young people of today, for whom some of these topics will be less of an issue. Until that day, we have to keep up the fight," said Sherman. ⊗

Jan Fox is an actor and writer, based in Los Angeles.

The Folger Library's touring exhibition Shakespeare – Life Of An Icon – travels throughout the US in 2016. The African-American Shakespeare Company will perform Anthony and Cleopatra in May 2016

The Bard meets Bollywood

45(01): 18/21 | DOI: 10.1177/0306422016643001

This year India is expecting to add to its own canon of films based on Shakespearean themes and plotlines, but can filmmakers use the plays to circumvent strict, but ambiguous, censorship laws? **Suhrith Parthasarathy** reports

ARSHINAGAR, A RECENTLY released Bengali musical, portrays a Hindu-Muslim divide through a plot based on Shakespeare's Romeo and Juliet. The Indian filmmakers aren't the first to employ such a device and they won't be the last. But the use of Shakespeare nods at current politics – in this case, communal riots – and points to a developing trend in Indian cinema: drawing on Shakespeare to impart messages that might otherwise be considered somehow subversive.

"Arshinagar doesn't quite take direct aim at the state by using Shakespeare," said Koel Chatterjee, who researches Shakespeare and Indian cinema at Royal Holloway, University of London. "But I'm told the politics in Zulfikar [another film currently in production], based on two different Shakespeare plays, is much stronger, and far more explicit," Chatterjee told Index.

Zulfikar, a Bengali drama directed by Srijit Mukherjee, is based on Julius Caesar, and Anthony and Cleopatra. Hindi film Veda, based on Hamlet and directed by Onir, is also due for release later in 2016.

"Shakespeare is such a cultural icon in India that his plays remain hugely relevant here even today," said Chatterjee. "His stories lend themselves so well to adaptation, and we are seeing more and more Indian films being made, either loosely or wholly, based on his works."

For many years in India, Shakespeare, at least in popular media such as films, was treated with a great degree of reverence, almost as though his stories were to be "wrapped in cotton wool", Poonam Trivedi, a reader in English at Indraprastha College, University of Delhi, said. There was an element of sacrosanctity to Shakespeare that prevented his plays, as malleable as they were, from being adapted into films with any great creative rigour. This, however, may be changing.

"The younger generations of filmmakers are more prone to using Shakespeare to convey harder, and more political, themes, because we're no longer as stuck by any colonial hangover," Trivedi said. "There are so many ideas and statements in Shakespeare which can be used as a means for either dodging censorship or towards stating what might generally be considered offensive."

India has a long history of censoring films, often for rather feeble reasons. The Central

discussions with a number of producers who would simply not go anywhere near a story which questions the status quo. Today, it doesn't matter whether the film is based on Shakespeare or not."

Baradwaj Rangan, a film critic and deputy editor at The Hindu newspaper, said that few filmmakers have dared to put the theory to the test. "Haider is possibly the only Shakespearean adaptation that deals with intensely controversial political issues," he said. "If you look at Vishal Bhardwaj's previous movies that adapted Shakespeare, the themes that they dealt with – infidelity and underworld crimes – were not particularly contentious. They didn't ask any serious questions of the state."

Perhaps one day as more filmmakers use Shakespeare to tell stories of political purport and depth, and seek to question the state more critically, then India might see the real value in using a classical plot to further free speech and expression. And it isn't only formal government censorship that Shakespeare and the classics can help overcome.

"There is an element of high culture to using Shakespeare," said Peer, explaining the credibility the Bard can give to controversy. "Othello can be used very subversively, as can The Merchant of Venice. These are stories that can be adapted to talk about the rise of the right in Europe, or the refugee crisis, or the state of intolerance today in India.

These are stories that can be adapted to talk about the rise of the right in Europe, or the refugee crisis

To use Shakespeare may not be one's first thought as a filmmaker, but what his plays unquestionably give us is a brand value. It can potentially be used as a clever device to tell uncomfortable stories." ⊗

Suhrith Parthasarathy is based in Chennai, and is a regular writer for Index

---

and permanence to Shakespeare's stories. They break all barriers of geography. Romeo and Juliet has been told in so many different ways, and so many different times. That didn't stop me from making my own movie by adapting the play. I'm sure it can be done over and over again. The possibilities are infinite.

To what extent do you think Shakespeare can help circumvent censorship in India?
I'd say the answer depends on the kind of story that you make. I have told difficult stories before of communal harmony without using Shakespeare. I did it with Mr and Mrs Iyer [a story of love revolving around a communal strife in India] back in 2002. I could have easily made Arshinagar differently

without invoking Romeo and Juliet. So I don't think Shakespeare necessarily helps us get past the censors. It all depends on the context of your story.

Formal censorship by state authorities aside, do you think the use of Shakespeare can help gloss over what might otherwise be an uncomfortable story to tell?
Again, I would say this depends a little on the context of the story. But I can see adapting Shakespeare as being useful in those ways, certainly. There might be stories that are considered political, which might be difficult to tell, that can be expressed well through the lens of Shakespeare.   **SP**

Lifting the curtain on Zimbabwe

45(01): 22/24 | DOI: 10.1177/0306422016643002

Playwright **Elizabeth Zaza Muchemwa** looks at how dissenting voices in the theatre are silenced in her homeland, and how Shakespeare has slipped through the censors' net both on stage and in classrooms

IN A HIGH-SCHOOL classroom, 14-year-old students are reading Shakespeare's tragedy Julius Caesar. A teacher gives students the historical context in which play is written then leads them through a reading, dramatisation and discussion of the play. The teacher also gives and asks for examples of incidents and ideas from real life which might enable the students to relate to the play's themes. Shakespeare's texts are taught in high schools around Zimbabwe on the mandated curriculum from the government. On average, more than 100 students are reading Shakespeare in every high school in Zimbabwe. This is happening while contemporary local playwrights have had skirmishes with the law concerning the content of their own works.

Zimbabwe is a country with a difficult socio-economic and political environment. Keen on retaining power, the liberation government has devised ways of keeping dissenting voices silent. They have fostered Judeo-Christian values and patriarchal practices on society, adding to instruments such as the Censorship and Entertainment Act, Access to Information and Protection of Privacy Act, and the Public Order and Security Act, which are used as tools to impede and ban artistic expression. The censorship laws

in place are enacted as if purely to prohibit artistic expression that is deemed to be politically incorrect, of an improper sexual nature, or depicting any sexuality other than heterosexuality or anything that demeans national heroes.

Theatre in the Park, an artist-led initiative that leased a space in a public park in Harare, has had its plays banned. One such play is Super Patriots and Morons, which was performed in 2004, depicting a senile head of state who refuses to let go of the reins of power. The play was banned after it had had its full run at Theatre in the Park and performances in almost all 10 provinces of the country. It became the first official play to be banned in independent Zimbabwe.

Daves Guzha, who commissioned the play, told Index on Censorship of his experience: "I was shocked, disgusted and humoured by the ban ... We were told the play was likely to cause alarm and despondency ... Because when you create work, the first audience you want to see the work is that of home ... And you want to be able to use that work 10 years later as a measure to say, we were there then, and where are we now?"

Theatre in the Park hosted a performance of Othello in 2012 and the Globe Theatre's performance of Hamlet in 2015. In both

cases they didn't have difficulty securing censorship clearance and they weren't advised to change a line or two in the text, as has been the experience of some theatre makers. This year they will be staging Julius Caesar at the Theatre in the Park's newly built venue in Harare Gardens, and they are keen on seeing what surprises the text will bring them.

Discriminatory application of the law has also seen plays that were clearly anti-establishment not being banned, while in other cases artists are arrested on charges of criminal nuisance. With the birth of opposition politics in the late 1990s, protest theatre became a popular genre in Zimbabwe and saw the rise of new voices, including Mandisi Gobodi, Raisedon Baya and Blessing Hungwe, whose popularity came out

One banned play is Super Patriots and Morons, which depicts a senile head of state who refuses to let go of power

of the controversy surrounding their work. When Hungwe's play Lovers in Time was shown at a local festival in 2014, the organisers got into a fracas with purported agents of the law. They were angered by the representation of Mbuya Nehanda, an iconic spiritual leader of the first liberation struggle. They couldn't understand why Nehanda, whom they have since appropriated into a card-carrying member of the party posthumously, would be re-imagined as →

ABOVE: Actors Daves Guzha (right) and Mackey Tickeys in a scene from the 2004 production Super Patriots and Morons, the first play to be banned in independent Zimbabwe

→ a transgendered youth in modern-day Zimbabwe.

Shakespearean texts that have been studied over the years in Zimbabwean high schools include: King Lear, which saw a senile king making mistakes and seen as a commentary on state leaders who stay in power past their sell-by date; Julius Caesar, which pushes the idea of the people taking back the power and betrayal; Hamlet, which paints a picture of succession battles, and Twelfth

The Zimbabwean playwright needs to take back the space of dialogue

Night and As You Like It, which have homo-eroticism and some reversal of gender roles. All these themes would raise the censorious eyebrows of the state if tackled in a modern play. Could it be Shakespeare's texts are allowed because the language is considered archaic and as such cannot possibly have a bearing on the mind-set of the people it reaches?

Playwright and arts critic Raisedon Baya told Index that the exceptionalism over Shakespeare is something to welcome: "The censorship is more political than anything, used a tool to intimidate and instil fear … Usually it is the police or central intelligence officers who come and tell you cannot go on … when it comes to foreign texts like Shakespeare, they appear to be unworried about the content of the plays … With Shakespeare plays you can adapt the text to speak to local experiences … We need to embrace Shakespeare."

In a country where legislative leaders are given the titles of "father" and "mother of the nation", it becomes difficult to call them on their mistakes when you have been taught to never dishonour an elder by questioning them.

Disempowering a person starts with taking away their ability to think and speak for

themselves. Children learn to allow thought to enter the mind and escape in speech without reserve. With adulthood one would have been conditioned to believe that there are things that are not thought of, let alone put into speech. The laws are enforced in such a way the censored start doing the job of the censor. You and your neighbour become the watchers.

Young playwrights are fired up by the need to change their lived reality. They create, but often with a worry of what will happen to them after freely expressing themselves. Some would rather steer clear of volatile topics, leaving them with a straitjacketed view of society which stifles their creativity. Zimbabwean society has over the years built its own socio-religious and political taboos, which have become synonymous with the state power. Writers ought to be exposed to the understanding that most of these taboos foster harmful practices, marginalising and stereotyping particular groups, denying them their basic rights, silencing divergent views to the detriment of the nation, creating myths about our national history that produces disaffected and disconnected youth, and sanitising hate speech, as well as other forms of violence.

There is no doubt that the Zimbabwean playwright needs to take back the space of dialogue. There are great lessons to be had from Shakespeare's work; not just in the fact that his works have transcended time and place, but that 400 years after his death his ideas are inspiring new generations in a distant country in southern Africa, unchecked. ⊗

Elizabeth Zaza Muchemwa is a poet, playwright and theatre director from Zimbabwe. Her latest written work is a play, The Fourth Interrogation. She will be in residence at the West Yorkshire Playhouse this spring

Lend me your ears

45(01): 25/29 | DOI: 10.1177/0306422016643003

Leading director **Roberto Alvim** talks to **Claire Rigby** about why Julius Caesar is so relevant to Brazil's current politics

SOME OF THE world's greatest plays, says Brazilian theatre director Roberto Alvim, are defined by their status as enduringly relevant works of art because they relate to fundamental aspects of our shared humanity. He gives Ibsen's Ghosts as an example: "It's a treasure of humanity." But there are other similarly universal plays that would be better classified as urgent, said Alvim in an interview with Index. "Those are the works that relate directly to the historical moment in which we are living," he said. And according to Alvim, that's precisely the case, in Brazil in 2016, with Shakespeare's Julius Caesar.

A multi-award-winning director at the age of 43, and a highly respected figure in the world of arthouse Brazilian theatre, Alvim smokes cigarette after cigarette as he talks inside the closed, empty bar at Club Noir, the theatre he founded in São Paulo in 2008 with his partner, the actor Juliana Galdino.

In a Brazil seething with political intrigue, in which the impeachment proceedings currently facing President Dilma Rousseff are just the most visible tip of a profound turbulence which has gripped the country since her re-election in October 2014, Alvim's 2015 adaptation of Julius Caesar was inspired by a televised presidential debate he saw in the final days of the election campaign, in which centre-left Rousseff faced off against her centre-right opponent Aécio Neves. "I watched the debate as it became utterly polarised between Dilma and Aécio, and the famous clash between Mark Antony

and Brutus instantly came to mind," he said. "It was the idea that the same facts can be drawn in such completely different ways by the power of speech: the power of the word to reframe the facts, and its central importance in the political game."

It's what Julius Caesar is all about, said Alvim – and it raised fundamental questions about the intrinsic value of freedom of expression. "What's the point of freedom of speech if we are constantly bombarded with lies and untrue information – and if we are reproducing it?" he asked. "Take Rousseff – she made a number of statements about economic policy before the elections, then adopted a completely different, neoliberal economic policy afterwards."

Her discourse altered completely, he said – and it's a trait that's not confined to politicians. "We all change our discourse according to the historical moment, and according to the side we find ourselves on at any given time."

In an interview with the newspaper O Globo, Carmo Dalla Vecchia, one of the two actors in Alvim's Caesar, said he recalled reading the script and connecting with "the great question" it asked of each one of us: "At what point in my life have I altered what I was going to say in order to win myself a more favourable position?"

Club Noir's production Caesar: How to Construct an Empire is Alvim's own adaptation from Shakespeare's text. The actors Dalla Vecchia and Caco Ciocler →

→ play more than 20 parts between them, switching roles for each of the 12 scenes in the play, to the extent of each playing the same characters in different scenes. The actors' movements on the stripped-down, darkened set are minimal, so that the lines, and their voices, become everything.

"The word," said Alvim, "is the element that orders time, space and the feelings within each scene."

Technically, Alvim said, Brazil enjoys a level of freedom of speech today that is vastly improved compared to other times in its recent history. "We spent 20 years under military rule," he said. "We were under se-

It's easy to see how Julius Caesar, the most political of all Shakespeare's plays, made Alvim see parallels with Brazil's stormy political scene

vere censorship. Artists and intellectuals were arrested, tortured and exiled. Plays were banned, theatres raided.

"People can say what they want now, within the framework of theatre, literature or music, or on social media or wherever – how often is the president of the republic called corrupt, a thief, on Facebook?"

And yet, he said, there are problems beneath the surface relating to the quality of that speech, and of public discourse in general. He pointed to what he describes as a dumbing down of the mainstream print media in terms of Brazil's two biggest newspapers.

"Until a year ago, Folha de São Paulo had two theatre critics: one for art and experimental theatre, and one for commercial productions." Only the latter remains at Folha, he said, while Estado de São Paulo no longer has a theatre critic at all. He said, together

with ever-shorter articles on the arts, there is a drastic narrowing of public discourse.

"The vocation of newspapers worldwide has always been not to follow the herd, not to follow the current, but to point to stronger, civilising instances," he said. And theatre, he believes, is the kind of work in which multiple viewpoints converge in contradictions. "It's essential. Since the birth of drama in 5th-century Greece, the theatre has been a place for deep discussion of issues concerning the entire polis."

It's easy to see how the issues and characters in Julius Caesar, the most political of all Shakespeare's plays, resonated for Alvim, and made him see parallels with Brazil's stormy political scene. The conspirator Cassio, with his "lean and hungry look", as Caesar describes him, the man who "thinks too much" is a dead ringer for the speaker of Brazil's congress, Eduardo Cunha, Rousseff's

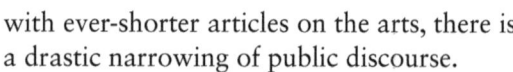

Credit: Leekyung Kim

arch-enemy and the driving force behind her impeachment. And though Rousseff herself, beset by difficulties, including a badly faltering economy, is far from "bestriding the narrow world like a Colossus", she is easily compared with Caesar in his final days – criticised, distrusted and perhaps, like Caesar, eventually eliminated from power by an excess of enemies on all sides.

In an act-two soliloquy (Scene IV, in Alvim's adaptation) as Brutus, the play's "honourable man", attempts to justify what he has already decided to do to his friend, he conjures up grounds for the pre-emptive reining-in of Caesar's possible future despotism, likening him to an unhatched serpent, to be killed in its shell. Power can lead people to great arrogance, muses Brutus. "So Caesar may. Then, lest he may, prevent."

The similarities with today's Brazil are many. An impeachment process has been launched against Rousseff because she is said to have violated budget laws to increase spending during her re-election campaign. She is not accused of the kind of personal corruption which has tainted dozens of Brazilian politicians – among them Cunha. Yet, Alvim said: "The president is constantly called corrupt. But there is no evidence of that whatsoever." What there is instead, he said, is a "very profound hatred" of Rousseff. Political decisions by voters, he said, are more often than not made on emotional, affective grounds. "Politics has little to do with rationality and reason, and that's also central to Julius Caesar," he said, citing the famous speech by Mark Antony in which he rouses the crowd to mutiny by force of clever rhetoric. "There is not a single concrete idea in that speech," he said. "Just production, rhetoric, cathartic emotion."

Allowing that kind of emotional →

ABOVE: Actors Caco Ciocler and Carmo Dalla Vecchia played 20 parts between them in Roberto Alvim's 2015 production of Julius Caesar

response to come to the fore in politics, he said, prevents relevant change from taking place. "It just generates more barbarism." Following Caesar's assassination, Alvim notes, comparing it to the danger of Rousseff's impeachment, the Roman Empire tumbled into civil war. He said: "It triggered a process of the dissolution of the state's democratic basis in a much worse manner than during Caesar's rule."

Luiz Inácio Lula da Silva, Rousseff's predecessor as president, was the target of similarly speculative fears during his presidency and beyond, said Alvim. "You hear it all the time, even now. Lula wants to turn Brazil into a communist republic. He wants Brazil to become another Venezuela. The same was said of Julius Caesar: 'He wants to become a tyrant.' But it's the projection of a fear, the

The conspirator Cassio, with his "lean and hungry look", is a dead ringer for the speaker of Brazil's congress

shadow of their own fears cast on him, with very little basis in fact." In government, argued Alvim, Lula made countless agreements with large corporations and all the main banks. "He was actually the most neoliberal president Brazil has ever had," he said.

Describing himself as left-wing, Alvim is nevertheless not an obvious supporter of the ruling Workers' Party, and has spoken vehemently against what he describes as the "Marxist mafia" or "cartel" in charge of allocating public funds for São Paulo theatre productions over the past few years, under which Club Noir and a number of other companies were excluded, he explained, from accessing funding over a period of almost three years. Club Noir's failure to win funding amounted, said Alvim, to a form of financial censorship. "We put on plays by

playwrights like Kafka, Pinter, Beckett, Ibsen, Genet," he said. "Our work is political, but not in the sense of being pamphleteering or partisan; and so it is dismissed as bourgeois, elitist." Year after year, the same theatre companies won funding. "Companies that basically just do Brecht, and theatre slanted in favour of a communist revolution. Not even they believe in it," he said. "It's just a way of defending their territory, and their funding."

Alvim's complaint led to a change in the rules, and the awarding commission now changes every six months. The good thing, said Alvim, is that such things can be reported and corrected these days, in contrast with the years of Brazil's last military dictatorship, from 1964 to 1985. Under that regime, countless theatre productions were censored. Musicals like Freedom, Freedom, received 25 cuts, and a production in Rio de Janeiro of Shakespeare's The Taming of the Shrew, also received line cuts. Plays like The Invasion, by Alfredo de Freitas Dias Gomes, and Tennessee Williams's A Streetcar Named Desire were banned completely.

Repression in the theatre reached a peak in 1968, when a production of the Chico Buarque play Roda Viva at São Paulo's Teatro Ruth Escobar was attacked by some 20 members of the paramilitary CCC – the Communist-Hunting Command (Comando de Caça aos Comunistas). Armed with guns, batons, hammers and knuckledusters, the group terrorised the audience and the cast before storming backstage, where they attacked the actors and stripped some of the women, forcing one woman and a man into the street, naked.

According to a 1992 account of the period by writer, actor and director Fernando Peixoto, there was a growing sense of moral outrage on the part of audiences, as well as the authorities. Audience members actually stood up and insulted actors during some productions. For Alvim that individual behaviour, beyond the acts of leaders, whether democratically elected or despotic, is also at

LEFT: Award-winning Brazilian theatre director Roberto Alvim was inspired to put on Julius Caesar after watching a televised presidential debate

2014 Bienal de São Paulo and last year's Venice Biennale for what he sees as their heavy-handed political pamphleteering. "The works had no aesthetic complexity," he said, noting an overwhelming number of works at both biennials denouncing things like sexism, racism, even paedophilia. "I don't need biennials to tell me about those things," he said. "I can read about them in articles and books." Art's true calling, he said, is deeper and more complex. "It's to help us to perceive the structural workings of things – to discover and reinvent our humanity, and how we relate to one another."

Club Noir's production of Caesar, which Alvim describes as an "aesthetic, emotional immersion", opened in São Paulo in July 2015 before touring Brazil. The production will transfer in February and March 2016 to Rio de Janeiro, and then there will be a handful of additional performances, including in Brasília, the seat of Brazilian government. A performance might just coincide, said Alvim, with the dreaded Ides of March (15 March) – and that might also, depending on how quickly things move, coincide with part of the impeachment process.

Beyond that, coming up at Club Noir in 2016 are productions of Spilt Milk, Alvim's adaptation of an acclaimed novel by Chico Buarque; Ibsen's Peer Gynt; and Shakespeare's Coriolanus. "Coriolanus is another perfect fit for our times," he said. "Coriolanus is given the duty to fight; and he fights. But once his bloodlust is stirred, it's impossible to stem the urge to violence and destruction." He compared it to Rio de Janeiro, where militias formed by members of the military police have carried out hundreds of extra-judicial executions. "They entered the military police to do justice," he said. "But once they start killing, how do you kill that urge?" ✺

Claire Rigby writes regularly for Index from São Paulo, Brazil, where she also reports for the Los Angeles Times, The Guardian and Vice News

the heart of Julius Caesar, and of Brazil in 2016. The lynching of the poet Cinna in the play, simply for having the same name as one of the conspirators, is comparable, he said, to a series of mob attacks that have taken place in Brazil in recent years, and to one incident at an anti-Rousseff demonstration in December, in which a young black boy of no more than 12 was filmed as a crowd of ostensibly upright citizens attempted to lynch him, slapping and hitting him. The video was shared widely and denounced on Brazilian social networks.

"In this era of global exchange," said Alvim, "where everybody has a platform to express their opinions, the strange thing is that we see fewer and fewer opinions, and fewer individual world views." Too many of us, he said, become trapped in polarised positions borrowed from others – ideas picked up on the internet and then "ventriloquised, repeated, like pirates' parrots". He said: "What we should be fighting for is freedom of 'impression' – the freedom to see the world in a detached way and to form our own impressions, so that when we open our mouths to speak, we are able to say something independent, emancipated and singular."

The role of art, in his view, is to equip people to be able to do just that. "A work of art doesn't exist to convince anyone of anything," he said. "It's a question of emancipation, of autonomy." He rails against the

Plays, protests and the censor's pencil

45(01): 30/35 | DOI: 10.1177/0306422016643005

Shakespeare was no stranger to censorship from the Elizabethan and Jacobean police states. Actor and writer **Simon Callow** charts how Shakespeare's plays have amused monarchs and dictators but also prompted their anger

WHEN I WAS at drama school in the early 1970s, there was a middle-aged Iranian on the directors' course called Rokneddin. He'd been ejected from the Shah's Iran for staging subversive productions. Rokneddin was no political firebrand: he had simply tried to put on Shakespeare's history plays, which, like all plays in which a king died, were banned in Iran under the Pahlavi dynasty. The plays reminded people all too vividly that the divine right of kings had severe limits.

After the revolution Rokneddin went back, and tried to ply his trade again: this time he disappeared into prison, never to be seen again. At the time the Shah's proscription was seen as the act of an exotic tyrant. That is not to say the English monarchy has always celebrated Shakespeare's entire canon. During the period of George III's madness in 18th-century Britain, King Lear was banished from the stage because the parallels were too obvious.

Shakespeare has had this unique symbolic significance for a long time. From the end of the 17th century, initially in England, and then increasingly in translation across Europe, his stock began its inexorable rise, until he was acclaimed across the whole of the Western world, to a degree never before or

since equalled by any other writer. His work was a mirror in which people of widely diverse cultures could see themselves – in Scandinavia, in the Middle East, in Spain and the Americas.

He was fervently admired in France, despite his barbaric non-conformism to the laws of classical drama. In Germany and Russia, he was clasped to those nations' bosoms, claimed by them as, respectively, German and Russian. Shakespeare's perceived universality – which expanded in the 19th and 20th centuries to include Africa, India, China and Japan – inevitably meant that his work would be recruited to embody the

positions of various political and philosophical groupings. And with this came, equally inevitably, censorship and suppression.

Not that Shakespeare was a stranger to censorship in his own time, living and working as he did in, first, the Elizabethan, then the Jacobean, police state where people's actions and their very thoughts were under constant surveillance. The theatre in which he worked was heavily patrolled by the Master of the Revels, who was charged not only with providing entertainment for the monarch, but with averting controversy, particularly in the sphere of foreign relations. Sometimes this meant deleting matters →

ABOVE: Actor Simon Callow playing the Master of the Revels in the 1998 film Shakespeare in Love

offensive to allies, sometimes it meant suppressing criticism – or perceived criticism – of the crown, sometimes, more rarely, it meant eliminating morally or sexually offensive material. The theatre was a minefield of significance for dramatists and their companies. Even a simple dig at German and Spanish dress had to be cut from Much Ado About Nothing because of contemporary

During George III's madness in 18th-century Britain, King Lear was banished from the stage

diplomatic sensitivities. But the reach of the censor went well beyond the explicit. The characters and narratives in Shakespeare's plays were perceived symbolically, as commentaries on current events.

In 1601 Shakespeare and his company, the Lord Chamberlain's Men, ran into danger on this account: the Earl of Essex and his supporter, the Earl of Southampton, Shakespeare's patron and possibly his lover, were planning a rebellion against the ageing Queen. They decided that it would help to rally support if Shakespeare's old play about a wayward despot, King Richard II, were to be revived. Comparisons between Richard and Elizabeth were common – even the Queen knew about them.

"I am Richard II, know ye not that?" she said to the keeper of records. "This tragedy," she continued, raging against the players' apparent impunity, "was played 40 times in open streets and houses." For the 1601 revival, the company really went out on a limb, adding the famous scene, possibly specially commissioned for the occasion, in which the king abdicates and is deposed. For their pains, the actors, including Shakespeare, found themselves arraigned by the Privy Council. Any one of them, including Shakespeare, could have been imprisoned for life,

like Southampton, or, like Essex, beheaded. In the end they got off on the shaky plea that they were just doing their job. The rebellion, of course, had failed abjectly. Had the rebellion succeeded, it might have been a different matter.

After Shakespeare's death, his plays were subjected to a different, internal, sort of censorship: on moral grounds, or those of taste. Happy endings were imposed, filth extirpated, difficult characters, like the fool in Lear, excised. But by the end of the 19th century, theatrical reformers had begun to establish the wildly controversial idea that Shakespeare might have known what he was doing. Almost immediately after this revelation directors began to use the plays to make points about the modern world. Especially in the wake of World War I, the martial dimension of the plays was subjected to intense scrutiny, and Shakespeare's patriotism was rarely taken at face value, until World War II, when, in Olivier's famous film, Henry V again became a rallying cry. But post-war productions have once again used the plays as a retort in which to examine our present preoccupations: Peter Brook's bleak absurdist King Lear, for example; Peter Hall's grimly realistic The Wars of the Roses; Jonathan Miller's Alzheimer's-stricken King Lear. Devastating truths have been confronted, but subversion has rarely been attempted.

Elsewhere, however, the plays have been keenly probed for political endorsement, or denounced for its absence. In 1941, Joseph Stalin banned Hamlet. The historian Arthur Mendel wrote: "The very idea of showing on the stage a thoughtful, reflective hero who took nothing on faith, who intently scrutinized the life around him in an effort to discover for himself, without outside 'prompting,' the reasons for its defects, separating truth from falsehood, the very idea seemed almost 'criminal'." Having Hamlet suppressed must have been a nasty shock for Russians: at least since the times of novelist and short story writer Ivan Turgenev,

LEFT: A production of Richard II ran into controversy in 1601. Here Nigel Lindsay (Bolingbroke) and David Tennant (Richard) star in a Royal Shakespeare Company production from 2013

the Danish Prince had been identified with the Russian soul. Ten years earlier, Adolf Hitler, had claimed the play as quintessentially Aryan, and described Nazi Germany as resembling Elizabethan England, in its youthfulness and vitality (unlike the allegedly decadent and moribund British Empire). In his Germany, Hamlet was reimagined as a proto-German warrior. Only weeks after Hitler took power in 1933 an official party publication appeared titled Shakespeare – A Germanic Writer.

As the Nazi newspaper Der Stürmer asserted: "If the courtier Laertes is drawn to Paris and the humanist Horatio seems more Roman than Danish, it is surely no accident that Hamlet's alma mater should be Wittenberg." A leading magazine of the time interpreted Hamlet's being denied his inheritance as a prefiguring of the Treaty of Versailles, and compared Gertrude's behaviour to that of Weimar's spineless politicians. When Britain declared war on Germany, Shakespeare was exempt from the ban on foreign playwrights because he was considered a German, even classic, author. In 1937, a production of Richard III was staged with a club-footed Richard, unmistakeably modelled on Joseph Goebbels. Soldiers were attired in Nazi uniforms, and the ghosts who

haunt Richard the night before Bosworth Field were openly compared to Hitler's victims in the Night of the Long Knives.

The comedies remained very popular. The Merchant of Venice was broadcast shortly after Kristallnacht and then given a splendid stage production in Vienna in 1943 to celebrate the city's being officially rid of Jews. Werner Krauss as Shylock made the audience shudder, "with a crash and a weird train of shadows, something revoltingly alien and startlingly repulsive crawled across the

In 1937, a production of Richard III was staged with a club-footed Richard, unmistakeably modelled on Goebbels

stage."

It is a measure of the extraordinary potency of the plays that such different regimes feel obliged to remake Shakespeare in their own image, to force the plays to toe the party line. Shakespeare cannot be ignored, so he must be made to conform. But it is equally a tribute to Shakespeare's own lack of censoriousness that the transformation →

is so easily effected. As with The Bible, you can prove almost anything from Shakespeare. His job was to capture life, not to judge it, and he succeeded triumphantly, but what must it have cost him? He endured enormous pressure from the censors, which seems to be reflected in a line from the great Sonnet 66 of which the first line is: "Tired with all these, for restful death I cry". In it, among the oppressions Shakespeare lists, he speaks in a great resonant line of: "art, made tongue-tied by authority".

All Shakespeare's working life the Master of the Revels, responsible for licensing every play performed in England, was Edmund Tilney. Early in Shakespeare's career, Tilney was involved in rewriting and censoring a highly contentious play. It was on the subject of Sir Thomas More, beheaded, of course, by Elizabeth's father, Henry VIII, and therefore a hot potato politically. We have one of the speeches it is believed that Shakespeare wrote for the play, the only surviving manuscript in his own hand. It is one of the finest things he ever wrote. More's plea on behalf of the migrants was written against a background of anti-immigrant riots in London. Its astonishing timeliness reminds one of why Shakespeare endures eternally, speaking to all of mankind. This is Thomas More's

|||||||||||||||||||||||||||||||||||||||||||||||||||||||||||||||||||||||||||||||||||||||||||||||||||||||||||

The play's the thing

··

KATHLEEN E. MCLUSKIE looks at how Shakespeare managed to steer clear of conflicts with the censors

In the earliest texts of Richard II, the scene in which the king is formally stripped of his crown does not appear. It might be assumed that it was excised from the text because of the political anxiety about Elizabeth's succession and this view gains support from the story that Shakespeare's company was invited – against their better judgement – to perform the play on the eve of the Earl of Essex's attempted coup. Members of Shakespeare's company were questioned about that performance but no harm came to them: they were just doing their job and the play was an old one that had been performed before. Within days of Essex's trial, they were playing at court again and the deposition scene was printed in the 1608 text, as well as in the Folio of Shakespeare's collected works.

It is impossible to tell whether the "deposition scene" had been performed all along and simply cut from the text by a nervous publisher; whether the Master of the Revels, whose job it was to protect the court from offence and the playwrights from official disapproval, had insisted it be cut; or indeed, whether Shakespeare had second thoughts about the emotional development of the play and wrote one of his most poetically powerful confrontations for the new edition.

We certainly have one very powerful example of Shakespeare's ability to work with the censor to try to keep a good play on the stage. In the unique censored copy of the play Sir Thomas More, amid the muddle of different contributors to the play and passages marked for cutting, there is a passage by Shakespeare written to re-work a censored scene in which Londoners stage an anti-immigration riot. Master of the Revels Edmund Tilney had clearly instructed the authors to "leave out the insurrection" and, to cover the missing material, Shakespeare provided a poetic plea from Sir Thomas More to the rebels. The speech asked them to imagine "the wretched strangers/Their babies at their backs with their poor luggage/ plodding to the ports and coasts for transportation". His speech insisted that disorder only endorsed further disorder where "men like ravenous fishes/Would feed on one another".

speech, first demanding order be restored:

Grant them removed, and grant that this your noise
Hath chid down all the majesty of England

And then to the rioters themselves:

Imagine that you see the wretched strangers,
Their babies at their backs, with their poor luggage
Plodding to the ports and coasts for transportation,
And that you sit as kings in your desires,
Authority quite silenced by your brawl
And you in ruff of your opinions clothed.
What had you got? I'll tell you: you had taught
How insolence and strong hand should prevail,

How order should be quelled, and by this pattern
Not one of you should live an agèd man,
For other ruffians, as their fancies wrought
With selfsame hand, self reasons and self right,
Would shark on you, and men like ravenous fishes
Would feed on one another.

The speech was never spoken, the play never heard: Tilney banned it. Art once again tongue-tied by authority. ⊗

Simon Callow is an actor, director and writer His latest book is Orson Welles: One Man Band (Jonathan Cape). He played Mr Tilney in the film Shakespeare in Love

||||||||||||||||||||||||||||||||||||||||||||||||||||||||||||||||||||||||||||||||||||||||||||||||||||||||||||||||||||||||||||||||||

The case that Shakespeare makes here and elsewhere against violent disorder may not tell us anything about his personal view of the regulation and censorship of drama in Elizabethan England. In the absence of other evidence, however, we might conclude that he was content to write the plays and manage the company with very little sense of how important his works would later be in providing eloquent justifications for the causes of freedom.

The familiar modern pattern of censorship – in which writers and artists bravely find ways to express subversive opinions in the face of dangerous reprisals from the state or religious authorities – cannot really be applied to the ramshackle system of regulation and control of theatre that existed in Shakespeare's time. Formally, there existed a variety of proscriptions – against writing English history, or dealing with religion, or representing a living monarch – but they were ignored by many playwrights, including Shakespeare.

From time to time, of course, the authorities of crown and church responded with vicious and summary brutality – pamphleteer John Stubbs lost his hand, writer William Prynne lost his ears and the dramatist Ben Jonson was thrown in jail over his controversial play Isle of Dogs. But far more

often during the Shakespearian period, from the 1580s to the 1620s, fierce threats to close the theatres once and for all or to call writers to be questioned by the Privy Council of the royal court dwindled into inaction: the offended nobleman was mollified, the period of political anxiety passed on; the delicate balance of support and control, on which courtly entertainment and a growing print and theatre industry depended, remained in place.

On the whole, and unlike some other dramatists, Shakespeare kept clear of controversy. There is scant evidence that his plays caused any official disquiet and concern is only identifiable through odd inconsistencies in the texts of his plays.

The censors cared about sedition, treason, religious and political dissent, but plays were censored more for insulting particular individuals, not so much for big ideas. Shakespeare's talent was to deal with big ideas in the context of human dilemmas that allows them to be applied to contemporary politics.

Kathleen E. McLuskie is emeritus professor of Shakespeare Studies and an honorary fellow of the Shakespeare Institute

Morals made to measure

45(01): 36/37 | DOI: 10.1177/0306422016643016

With its arranged marriages, death sentences and bans on frivolity, Shakespeare's Measure for Measure has new relevance if you replace the 17th-century Puritans with Islamists. **Tom Holland** argues for an updated version for our times, set in the Middle East

"**D**OST THOU THINK,** because thou art virtuous, there shall be no more cakes and ale?" So Sir Toby Belch, in Twelfth Night, famously skewers the Puritan steward, Malvolio. Perilous though it is to ascribe with confidence any views on religion to Shakespeare, it is reasonable to assume that Belch's hostility towards the finger-wagging quality of Puritan moralising reflected something of the playwright's own. Certainly, the humiliations visited on Malvolio – tricked into thinking that his mistress is in love with him, and conned into making a fatal fashion faux pas – do not show his taste for virtue-signalling in a good light. "I'll be revenged on the whole pack of you!" he vows, once his gullibility has been exposed. It is the very last thing he says beforing exiting the stage in impotent fury.

What, though, if a man like Malvolio were to be, not a servant, but a master, and provided with the reins of state? The question was to prove more than hypothetical: for by 1650, Puritans would indeed have seized control of England, and banned both plays and Christmas cake. Shakespeare himself, a couple of years after writing Twelfth Night, offered his own exploration of what Puritanism might look like if it came to power, when

he wrote another comedy: Measure For Measure. The play is set in Vienna, and begins when its duke, temporarily abdicating, entrusts the rule of the city to Angelo, a man who – like Malvolio – makes an ostentatious display of his own virtue.

"Were he meal'd with that
Which he corrects, then were he tyrannous;
But this being so, he's just."

Yet Angelo does not prove just. Even as he presides over the clean-up of Vienna, a city rotten with syphilis and prostitution, he succumbs to the very lusts that he is punishing in others. Isabella, the sister of a man condemned to death for extra-marital sex, comes to him to beg for her brother's life; and Angelo, overwhelmed by desire for this unexpected supplicant, attempts to seduce her. Compounding his hypocrisy is that Isabella's chastity could not be more clearly advertised: for she wears the habit of a nun. The display of her purity, though, only excites the hitherto pious Angelo all the more. The bargain he proposes is an impossible one: her brother's head in exchange for her maidenhead.

All along, though, the Duke has been secretly on hand to set things right. At the end of the play, he casts off the disguise he has

been wearing for the past five acts, and exposes Angelo in his turn.

"I am sorry, one so learned and so wise
As you, Lord Angelo, have still appeared,
Should slip so grossly."

Such a climax is, of course, very much in the grand tradition of English literature. From Chaucer's Pardoner to Dickens' Mr Pecksniff, many of its most memorable characters have been monuments to hypocrisy. Angelo's downfall, though, does not raise much of a smile. Written at much the same time as Othello, a play which takes the tropes of comedy and transforms them into tragedy, Measure For Measure is a comedy shot through with a sense of the tragic. While Angelo's hypocrisy is that of the theocracy that he aspires to impose upon Vienna, the city is left no less criminal and syphilitic for his exposure. "Like doth quit like," the Duke declares ringingly at the end of the play, "and Measure still for Measure" – but the play is vastly more ambivalent than this implies. Between licence and order – or between liberty and repression, depending on one's perspective – there can ultimately be no compromise. Society offers nothing but two rotten extremes.

The unsettling potency of this vision has not lost its ability to fascinate modern audiences, who, rather than being put off by the status of Measure For Measure as one of Shakespeare's "problem plays", have tended instead to revel in it. Nevertheless, it is hard to avoid the suspicion that its impact, in countries where theocracy is no longer a viable prospect, and permissiveness has been enshrined almost as a moral good, stands somewhat diminished. What, though, if its setting were to be transferred from Vienna to a city in the Middle East – one where playboys drive their sports cars past Islamists yearning for sharia? Isabella, whose defence of her chastity can often make her appear neurotic and unreasonable to secular audiences, would seem altogether more convincingly agonised as a hijabi.

LEFT: Isabella (Mariah Gale) pleads with Angelo (Kurt Egyiawan) in a 2015 performance of Measure for Measure at London's Globe theatre

"What's this? What's this? Is this her fault or mine?" So Angelo asks himself, as he contemplates his desire for her. "The tempter, or the tempted, who sins most?"

A world where women are condemned for provoking lust in men; where those who fall foul of self-appointed moral arbiters risk decapitation; where arranged marriages are taken for granted: such was the one that Shakespeare portrayed in his most morally ambivalent play. Remote though it may seem to most Western audiences, it no longer, perhaps, appears quite as remote as it might have done a few years back. Touching as it does on topics so taboo that even the boldest contemporary dramatist might think twice

What if its setting were to be transferred from Vienna to a city in the Middle East – one where playboys drive their sports cars past Islamists yearning for sharia

before exploring them, the play constitutes startling testimony to the enduring ability of Shakespeare to seem our contemporary. Fingers crossed, we will see an Islamised Measure For Measure soon. ⊗

Tom Holland's latest book is Dynasty, a history of Rome's first imperial dynasty. He is also the presenter of BBC Radio 4's Making History

The writer of our discontent

45(01): 40/43 | DOI: 10.1177/0306422016643018

Hungarian author and dramatist **György Spiró** looks at the role Shakespeare has played in challenging eastern European dictators

WHAT HAPPENED TO me in 1979 is characteristic of the Hungarian cult of Shakespeare. I had brought back from England close to 40 books written in Russian, Polish, Czech and English. Not one of them was in Hungarian. I travelled by train, and during customs checks, all the books were confiscated, except one: after some hesitation, the officer returned a one-volume complete Shakespeare, in English, even though, as far as I was concerned, this was the most subversive work of all.

From the beginning of the 19th century, Hungarian theatre-goers have considered William Shakespeare to be the most popular Hungarian author. At first, he was translated from the German version, but later the greatest Hungarian poets of the Romantic era, Mihály Vörösmarty, János Arany and Sándor Petőfi, translated him directly from English.

Yet, with the exception of a handful of extraordinary performances, in times of political repression in Hungary, cultural figures did not censor Shakespeare. They censored through Shakespeare.

Hiding behind his name and works, theatre managers engaged in self-censorship. When they were too afraid to deal with

current topics, they would turn to the safety of Shakespeare or Anton Chekhov, who were both deemed acceptable. I am a fervent admirer of the two literary giants, but I must admit that in today's Hungarian theatres they are used as tools of evasion.

All sorts of startling, supposedly original, ideas have been tried out on stage – swapping scenes around, splicing in works of other authors, using modern weapons or motorcycles – but these innovations have very little to do with Hungarian reality, or with what Shakespeare may have really meant. Critics praise the performances, or pan them, and the profession makes believe that something important has happened.

One of the most highly anticipated recent performances was Julius Caesar by prominent director Róbert Alföldi at Budapest's largest theatre, the Vígszínház, in 2014. Alföldi was previously director of the National Theatre, during which time some critics reviled him for being gay and demanded from him greater reverence for 19th-century romantic nationalism. When his contract at the National Theatre was not renewed in 2013, quite a few actors left in protest. Yet, unfortunately, his recent Julius Caesar did not satisfy any overarching political expectations: it did not criticise the rulers of Hungary enough, nor did it pander enough to the conservatism of theatre regulars. Despite containing a few fine ideas, the play had a rather short run.

Throughout the 20th century, dictators were readily depicted in eastern Europe through Shakespeare's plays. In the 1955 revival of Richard III at Budapest's National Theatre, spectators were reminded of the machinations of Mátyás Rákosi, Hungary's Stalinist dictator. Tamás Major, then director of the National Theatre, assumed the play's title role. The production had premiered in 1947, when Rákosi was not yet a dictator. In the intervening years, one or two actors had passed away, a few had joined other companies, but the rest of the players and the

staging remained the same. However the audience's reaction in 1955 was different: the scrivener's lines in the sixth scene of act three were greeted by wild applause, an outburst which had not been noted in 1947.

Scrivener: ... Who is so gross
That cannot see this palpable device?
Yet who so bold but says he sees it not?
Bad is the world and all will come to nought,
When such ill dealing must be seen in thought.

It is said that Mihály Farkas, then minister of defence, ran up to the director's office and took offence at seeing the audience demonstrating against Rákosi's régime. To which Tamás Major supposedly responded: "I must say, Comrade Farkas, that only you could come up with such idiotic nonsense." A wise dictator pretends not to notice any of this. Tamás Major remained as director, and the audience was happy to see the dictator and his system in a light that contemporary authors wouldn't dare describe.

Richard III was staged in Kaposvár which had the country's very best theatre at the time. This was 1982. The superb actors wore

In times of political repression in Hungary, cultural figures did not censor Shakespeare. They censored through Shakespeare

camouflage military uniforms, and the action took place behind prison bars. At the end of the performance, Richmond's speech was broadcast on closed-circuit television to the auditorium. A talented extra played the role of the obnoxious figure, but that wasn't why charges were brought against the production, they were brought because the Earl of Richmond wore dark glasses. A few weeks earlier, on 13 December 1981, General →

OPPOSITE: The bloodied cast of Julius Caesar, directed by Róbert Alföldi, at Budapest's Vígszínház theatre in 2014

→ Wojciech Jaruzelski declared a state of emergency in Poland. For health reasons he wore sunglasses every time he appeared in public.

László Babarczi, the director of the play, was reprimanded. He defended himself by stating that the actor did not wear sunglasses. After he was reported, the actor did indeed stop wearing them. Babarczi also argued that they began rehearsing the drama before the Polish putsch – the play had been added to the season schedule and approved by the ministry of culture. Later, the stage manager of the theatre, Tamás Ascher, had this to say: "It made no difference if he was wearing dark glasses or not. That wasn't the problem. Our mistake was thinking that every takeover [of power] works this way. But this one served neither the future nor justice itself. What it served was a base conspiracy. This was the crux of the matter." Our forebears in eastern Europe bequeathed to us the same lesson, in a German aphorism: *Es kommt selten was besseres nach* (What follows is rarely better).

Audiences acknowledged with some satisfaction that the Earl of Richmond – who

Charges were brought against the production, because the Earl of Richmond wore dark glasses – like Poland's General Jaruzelski

becomes Henry VII – is going to be just as debased as the recently murdered Richard III. For once, the audience did not long for an idyllic ending – it wanted to see the truth. The unique staging of the play would have had an effect on the spectators even if no dictatorship had been established in Poland.

As a literary adviser at the Kaposvár theatre, I agreed with the ending they chose, and 10 years later in a book of mine entitled Doubling in Shakespeare's Plays I dealt with

this very theme. A number of scholars, David Bevington, for instance, Thomas James King or Richard G. Mansfield, believe that in the Elizabethan age actors in leads never played dual roles. As far as I am concerned, in Shakespeare's dramas, even the protagonist can play another role within the same production. The same actor can be both Julius Caesar and Octavius – what's more, this could be the very essence of the tragedy of Julius Caesar. A dictator can be done away with, but the dictatorial function, once it's established, can never be abolished. In Richard III, which was written earlier, nothing prevents an actor from playing both Richard's and Richmond's part. In fact, the long scene near the end of the play, in which the ghosts talk now to Richard, now to Richmond, highlights the play's dramatic power. We're watching a bit of buffoonery. One minute the chief clown puts on his crown, and pretty soon he takes it off. When both are on stage, Richard has no lines. They engage in a little swordplay, then run off. In that era, substitution was a typical solution on stage. Richmond's speeches invariably have a double meaning, but if the same actor plays Richard, his words are even more equivocal.

Since then there has not been such a well-timed staging of Richard III. Most performances of the play indicate that there is an arch-villain with one or two helpers, and the rest are victims. There isn't a single production in which Richard III is only one cynical murderer among many such characters, even though Shakespeare strongly emphasises this state of affairs in the first scene. After the coronation, a child-like page is quick to round up professional killers, as requested by the king, though the page did not learn the ropes in Richard's reign, but well before, during the War of the Roses. The logic of war lives on, it's never-ending – this was Shakespeare's unalterable experience.

In 1962, six years after the Hungarian Revolution, a memorable new production

Credit: Wellesz Ella

of Hamlet opened in Budapest. Emulating Laurence Olivier, Miklós Gábor also wore a black, tight-fitting suit. Before the revolution, the well-known Hungarian actor had spread Stalinist dogma. The revolution shook him up, and from then on, he kept repenting. His Hamlet, from today's perspective, seems rather mannered. But at the time, the whole country recognised itself in the actor's vacillations, in his inner struggle. As a high-school student, I, too, was deeply moved.

In early November 1984, the Kaposvár Theatre made a guest appearance in Moscow, presenting Hamlet. I based the dubbed text on Boris Pasternak's Russian translation, from which the Russians had expunged Ophelia's naughty little ditties. Our production was precise, but cool. It wasn't a great hit at home either, even though it could boast a bunch of good thoughts. Director Tamás Ascher had come up with the idea that the mousetrap scene should be followed by a completely silent one, in which the actors were chased out of the Danish royal court. In Kaposvár, this little interlude depicted succinctly and effectively the relationship between artists and the powers that be.

That year, at Moscow's 7 November military parade, the airshow of fighter planes was cancelled. At this point the struggle between the leader of the Soviet Union, Mikhail Gorbachev, and the hardliners had not yet been resolved, and the bigwigs were afraid that a bomb might be planted on Red Square. The Hungarian actors, who didn't speak Russian, nevertheless felt the tension, and our somewhat sluggish home production unexpectedly became shot through with the atmosphere of the moment. I hadn't seen anything like it before or since. A receptive group of people in the audience somehow rearranged the production. Gábor Máté played Hamlet, and all of a sudden he gave one of the strongest interpretations I've ever seen. The first night the house was three-quarters full, but the next day there were long queues at the entrance. It seemed as if the entire Soviet avant-garde were trying to push their way in. During the performance a dozen comrades in suits and ties were nervously running around the lobby with earphones in their ears and the Russian text of Hamlet in their hands, trying to figure out what could we have added to that play to make it so popular all of a sudden, and what could they have banned if they had paid more careful attention.

In the past 30 years, censors in Hungary have not interfered with Shakespeare's texts. The censors considered Shakespeare an uninteresting author; some of his plays or excerpts from his dramas were compulsory reading in high school. Even then they found them flatly boring. From time to time, theatres that shine in oppositionist roles can send timely political messages. Fake blood flows amply on the stage. In Shakespeare's time they poured sheep's blood from goatskin. Nowadays the censors, while dozing off, smile over such silliness, and in their secret reports they probably write: "passé".

The main question has nothing to do with censorship. Our theatre language in the middle of the 20th century became more and more visual, while Shakespeare's language is more auditory. To change textual theatre into pictorial theatre is extraordinarily difficult. Which doesn't mean that it is impossible. In the theatre, anytime, anything is possible. ⊗

Translated by Ivan Sanders.

György Spiró is a Hungarian novelist, essayist and dramatist. His latest novel, Captivity, won an Aegon Literary Award, and has been translated and published by Restless Books (restlessbooks.com)

LEFT: Tamás Major playing the title role in Richard III at Budapest's National Theatre in 1955. Audiences were said to have drawn parallels with Mátyás Rákosi, Hungary's Stalinist dictator

Star-crossed actors

45(01): 44/46 | DOI: 10.1177/0306422016643019

When theatre makers in Kosovo and Serbia decided to put on a ambitious, dual-language production of Romeo and Juliet to tackle themes of feuding and reconciliation, **Preti Taneja** travelled to see the top-secret rehearsals and premiere

SHAKESPEARE'S ROMEO AND Juliet, with its theme of two families forced to bury an ancient grudge after a long feud, is resonant for the creators of a theatre project in Kosovo and Serbia, which is about to start a five-venue regional tour. The production is a ground-breaking collaboration that premiered at the National Theatre of Serbia in Belgrade in April 2015, and then at the National Theatre of Kosovo last May.

It was the first time since the bitter Balkan conflict ended in the late 1990s that a cultural production had been sponsored by the governments of both places, and shown with such prominence. Carefully composed of equal numbers of well-known actors and rising stars from both Serbia and Kosovo, with a script translated into both languages, the production's final secret ingredient was the choice of play itself. Shakespeare as a negotiator for change and reconciliation was at work here.

Yet, when Serbian actor and director Miki Manojlović approached Jeton Neziraj in Kosovo with the project, the founder of Pristina-based theatre company Qendra Multimedia was sceptical. He grew up in the 1990s, when Kosovo's Albanian community faced ethnic cleansing via cultural subjugation by Serb forces. They were prohibited from entering public life or having access to higher education and cultural institutions. The Albanian language was banned in schools and media. When these repressions led to war, thousands died and many more were displaced from their homes.

To Neziraj, the idea of doing Romeo and Juliet seemed too sentimental, too twee. He agreed partly because of the multilingual script, and the promise that actors from each side would perform in both Serbian and Albanian. But eventually he agreed, because, he said, "It's very ambitious. In terms of money, in terms of politics, in terms of people involved." Using Shakespeare, he felt, would send a message to the world beyond the Balkans about the potential for cultural

exchange in his war-scarred region. "This was a temptation to do something big," he said.

It's not the only Shakespeare production that has crossed barriers. In 2005 Bosnian director Haris Pašović brought together a cast from Bosnia, Serbia, Croatia and Slovenia, then took them on tour across the region. The play was Shakespeare's Hamlet. Like Manojlović and Neziraj's Romeo and Juliet, the production attracted the attention of international media, including The Guardian and The Times; testimony to the UK interest in how people outside the country "do" Shakespeare. The coverage speaks to a sense there that somehow Shakespeare remains an English playwright, even in translation. Perhaps the choice of Shakespeare

Using Shakespeare, he felt, would send a message to the world beyond the Balkans about the potential for cultural exchange in his war-scarred region

even influenced the major financial backers for Neziraj and Manojlović's project: as both places vie towards accession to the European Union, €130,000 ($142,000) came from the EU offices in both Serbia and Kosovo.

Other donors included the Open Society Foundation, the Ministry for Culture in Serbia and Kosovo's Ministry for Foreign Affairs. Given that Serbia does not even recognise Kosovo as an independent state, this is progress indeed. It was kept behind the scenes, however: the Serbian edition of the programme did not include the logo of the Republic of Kosovo (instead the liaison office of Kosovo in Belgrade was name checked).

I went to Pristina in February 2015 to meet Neziraj and find out how the production was coming together. From Skopje, the Macedonian capital, I took a six-hour →

OPPOSITE: The Montagues and the Capulets in Romeo and Juliet, produced by Qendra Multimedia and Radionica Integracije, at the National Theatre of Serbia in Belgrade

ABOVE: Romeo and Juliet in performance at the National Theatre of Serbia in Belgrade

bus ride across the border to Pristina. Neziraj met me at the bus station and showed me around the city while we talked: he warned that evening a demonstration would be taking place in the city's Mother Teresa Square. Sure enough, thousands of student protesters gathered to demand the release of Albanian prisoners from Serb prisons, and the unification of the town of Mitrovica, which has remained divided between Serbs and Kosovo Albanians since the bitter conflict between the two officially ended in the 1990s.

Montagues and Capulets moved along the stage, hissing sarcastic greetings in Serbian, in Albanian

The Teatri Kombëtar, the National Theatre of Kosovo, sits modestly at the top of a concrete flight of steps on the edge of the square, facing off with the parliament building: a hint at how political a battleground culture is here. The theatre was closed, but the glass tower of the National Assembly was pockmarked with holes, the glass smashed just weeks earlier by rocks and petrol bombs. A crowd of more than 2,000 people had clashed violently with police, protesting their government's climb down over a major mine that lies inside Kosovo's borders, but which is claimed by Serbia. Their anger was fuelled by anti-Albanian remarks made by ethnic Serb politician Aleksander Jablanovic (then minister of communities and returns, and member of the Kosovo parliament), who called a group of Kosovo Albanians "savages" when they blocked a pilgrimage of

Serbs trying to reach one of Kosovo's Orthodox Christian monasteries over Christmas. It was difficult to believe such a collaborative production could and would take place here.

From Pristina I had to travel back to Skopje to fly to Belgrade, as going over land would have rendered my entry into Serbia illegal. I was allowed into the top-secret rehearsals; then came back to see the premiere as it took place in both cities.

So, was it any good? A bare silver platform in the shape of a cross was built across the dark stage. Montagues and Capulets moved in packs along it, hissing sarcastic greetings in Serbian, in Albanian. The lovers gripped each other; Juliet as much a fighter wielding a knife, as she was an object of desire. Lady Montague soothed her Romeo with Albanian lullabies; the nurse was suitably coarse and knowing.

The action was gripping but foreknowledge of the coming tragedy saturated the audience, and was echoed in the body language of Benvolio, Mercutio and Tybalt as they fought with weapons and words. At the end, I saw audiences in Pristina and Belgrade stand to cheer; the actors stepped off the stage to shake hands with them. Nothing could mar the moment, not even the message, chalked at the foot of those concrete steps outside the theatre: "No Serbian Hoofs on the Kosovan Stage".

The show went on, despite a power cut which plunged everyone into darkness at the the next day's matinee. As the plans for a regional tour gather pace, the play might offer a space for audiences to reflect not only on the "ancient grudge" that continues to grieve communities and keep them divided, but also on the potential for reconciliation that collaboration through culture – in this case, through Shakespeare – can offer. ⊗

Preti Taneja is a research fellow in global Shakespeare at the University of Warwick/Queen Mary University of London, where she studies Shakespeare in conflict and post-conflict zones

THE PLACE TO BE FOR FAMILY THEATRE

UNICORN

THE UK'S THEATRE FOR YOUNG AUDIENCES

'One of the most exciting places to see theatre in the UK.'
Guardian

BOOKING NOW OPEN FOR SPRING SHOWS.

UNICORN THEATRE, 147 TOOLEY STREET, LONDON SE1 2HZ ⊖ ≷ LONDON BRIDGE
020 7645 0560 · UNICORNTHEATRE.COM
🐦 UNICORN_THEATRE f UNICORNTHEATRE ▶ UNICORNTHEATRE

Supported using public funding by
ARTS COUNCIL ENGLAND

Registered Charity No 225751

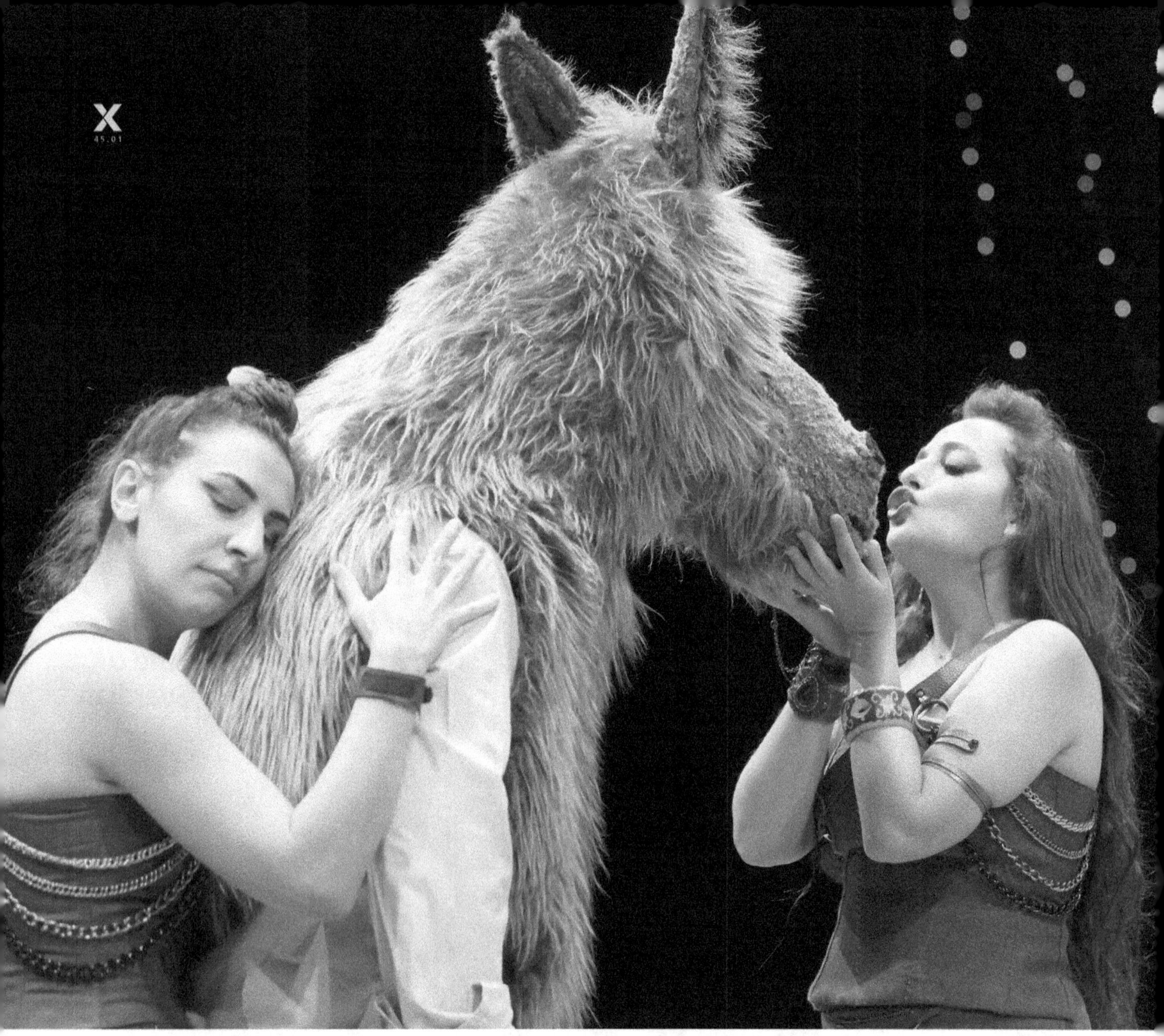

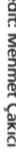

When the Dream upset the regime

45(01): 48/51 | DOI: 10.1177/0306422016643020

In 1981 actors appearing in a Turkish adaptation of A Midsummer Night's Dream ended up in jail and were subjected to psychological "retraining". **Kaya Genç** talks to a leading Shakespearian director about how the play still has political importance in Turkey today

Credit: Mehmet Çakıcı

ALMOST EXACTLY 35 years ago, months after the Turkish general staff had taken over the reins of political power through a bloody military coup, a theatre company based in Istanbul's Tepebaşı neighbourhood put on a new play: a Turkish adaptation of William Shakespeare's A Midsummer Night's Dream. The play was translated by Can Yücel, a Turkish poet known for his communist views and uncompromising attitude towards all kinds of authority.

This was no ordinary Shakespeare staging. Even before it was premiered there were rumours about the production's potential to serve as Yücel's commentary on the new military regime, a regime which had just started arresting young people who shared Yücel's politics. In 1981, any public event, newspaper article, poem or artistic production carrying even the slightest trace of dissent against the military authority was certain to be punished. It would be mad to stage a rebellion at the heart of Istanbul – but that is exactly what the Tepebaşı Experimental Theatre ended up doing.

Not long after the premiere in January 1981, Tepebaşı Experimental Theatre started having problems. Turkish citizens were being asked, and encouraged, to spy and inform on people they suspected of having "extremist" views. Arrests of political figures in Istanbul had become a daily occurrence; the coup resulted in the execution of 50 people, hundreds of deaths in prisons and the arrest of around half a million citizens.

Actors from the Tepebaşı Experimental Theatre experienced their share of trouble. Every other week a different actor would be arrested by the military police, sent to the Hasdal military barracks in Istanbul's Kağıthane neighbourhood. Once there, their heads would be shaved, they would be forced to live with prisoners who held opposite political views and asked to accept the statist-militarist ideology as their own. As a result of the arrests, numerous actors of the company were obliged to play multiple roles

in the remaining weeks of the run. Only 14 members of the original 22-strong cast survived the season as free citizens. The others ended up behind bars.

Located in Istanbul's touristic centre, 100 metres from Agatha Christie's favorite Istanbul hotel, the Pera Palace, the old theatre building is now a car park. Tepebaşı Experimental Theatre's staging of Midsummer

Only 14 members of the original 22-strong cast survived the season as free citizens. The others ended up behind bars

Night's Dream soon achieved a kind of cult status. "Director Başar Sabuncu had staged this play in a building resembling a warehouse; it was great entertainment," Turkish critic Fatih Özgüven wrote in his obituary for Sabuncu, who died in 2015. "This was the first half of the ominous Turkish 1980s. I remember how pleased people were with the wind that emanated from this production."

That wind can still be felt in the streets of Istanbul, today. In an interview with Index on Censorship, Kemal Aydoğan, the director of the latest Turkish adaptation of A Midsummer Night's Dream, described the work as "one of the most political plays ever written". For Aydoğan, the scene in which the Amazonian queen Hippolyta is subjugated and taken hostage by the Theseus marks a turning point in the play. "This is the point where matriarchy ends and patriarchy begins," he said. "That Hermia is not allowed to marry the man she loves but has to wed the man assigned to her by her father is another sign of women's subjugation by men." This, according to Aydoğan, is sadly familiar terrain for Turkey where women are frequently told by male politicians to know their place, keep silent and do what they are told by men. →

OPPOSITE: In Kemal Aydogan's 2015 Turkish adaptation of A Midsummer Night's Dream, Hippolyta (Didem Balcin) falls in love with the donkey-costumed Nick Bottom (Caner Erdem) and kisses him after being manipulated by the fairies

Aydoğan is fascinated by the artisan/actor characters in the play (known as the rude mechanicals in Shakespearean scholarship), who point to the class-based nature of Athenian society. "Dialogues between artisans give a good sense of the tyrannical nature of the state apparatus," Aydoğan said. "Theseus's tolerance towards the artisans is fake. The upper classes here see the lower classes merely as objects of entertainment. And then there is the forest, the locale of the unconscious, the desires, the fantasies, the classlessness, the spirituality... If patriarchy has the city and the state, then the female has the forest where there is no hierarchy between fairies who manage that world."

To make the production more experimental and interactive, Aydoğan's team built a round structure at Istanbul's Moda Sahnesi theatre. They placed the stage at the centre, so that members of the audience could surround the actors. When I went to watch this production I was able to observe the other spectators, as well as the actors, seated all round the theatre.

"The Globe theatre's architecture played a huge role in Shakespeare's works," Aydoğan said. "It was a 270-degree chamber, watched

This Shakespeare production had the potential to reflect Turkey's authoritarian climate in a way that would pass under the radar

by three levels of audience. This had a major influence on Shakespeare's aesthetics. People from different classes could co-exist there. We can call this structure the most perfect form of democracy, and it was this that we wanted to construct at Moda Sahnesi. We wanted our audience to surround us and see each other. We wanted to remove the distance between the actor and the audience, between life and art."

The formal and democratic nature of Shakespeare's work is something Aydoğan and his fellow dramatists at Moda Sahnesi care deeply about. Aydoğan is grateful for Turkish directors who came before him and adapted Shakespeare for Turkish audiences. He accepts that his Moda Sahnesi didn't have the kind of experience Tepebaşı Theatre actors had in 1981 and describes that production "a milestone".

"In the past 70 years, Shakespeare's most popular play, Antony and Cleopatra only had four different productions in Turkey. A Midsummer Night's Dream, meanwhile, was staged hundreds of times, under numerous productions whose dramatic approaches ranged from the traditional to the experimental," said Aydoğan. "The reason it became this popular was the way Yücel and the Tepebaşı Theatre crew adapted it to Turkey's oppressive atmosphere in the 1980s. They added a Turkish tone. From what I [heard from those] who had seen it, it was staged in an atmosphere of a rebellion. Before the 1981 production, Shakespeare was seen as an elite figure, who audiences felt they should keep away from and admire from afar. With Yücel's translation this changed completely. It gave rise to the birth of a more comprehensible, more human Shakespeare for Turkey's theatre-goers."

In the Turkey of 2016, Aydoğan found echoes of the Athenian conflict, pointing to the continuing struggle between what he calls "the forces of desire and law".

"In the forest of A Midsummer Night's Dream there is no divide between women and men. No social classes divide people there," he said. "In the play there is a struggle between desire and law. And that is the main feature of today's liberation struggles in Turkey. We all live at the bosom of the law while collectively desiring to reach our forests where we can dream of a society far placed miles away from the forces of law."

Perhaps it was this same conflict Yücel had identified a quarter of a century ago in

Istanbul, in the days following the worst military coup the country had seen. As a Marxist who believed in using all forms of culture to pursue his left-wing agenda, Yücel saw, in this Shakespeare production, the potential to reflect Turkey's authoritarian climate in a way that would pass under the radar of the military intelligence's hardworking censors. Like lovers in Shakespeare's comedy who are tricked by fairies into falling in love with characters they actually dislike, his adaptation drew on the idea that Turkey's people were forced by the state to love the authority figures that oppressed them the most. They were subjugated by the military patriarchy, the same way the play's female and artisan characters were subjugated by Athenian patriarchy. The class distinctions that are at the heart of Shakespeare's play (one group of its characters consists of a duke and other leading members of the Athenian aristocracy; the other group, made up of six amateur actors with working-class backgrounds) similarly defined life in Turkey and was the actual reason behind the coup. According to Yücel's Marxist reading, they desired to stifle all forms of working-class dissent.

Thanks to Yücel's localisation of Shakespeare's text – his translation featured numerous Istanbul references from the French school Notre Dame de Sion to the city's luxurious hotels and even included a Turkish character called Müezzen – the coup-shocked audience felt that this might well be a play about contemporary Turkey. There were additions to Shakespeare's text, with references to demagogues who, like the coup's ultra-nationalist leader general Kenan Evren, fooled the nation through their demagoguery.

Yet 35 years after the influential Tepebaşı production, I found myself sitting in an Irish pub on the Asian side of Istanbul, before seeing Aydoğan's production of A Midsummer Night's Dream for a second time and wondering whether the play might still inspire Turkey's theatre world into questioning their

country's status quo.

Before I paid for my pint, a group of protesters walked past the pub, chanting political slogans. They asked customers to "wake up" and pay attention to the things going on in Turkey's south-eastern cities. The escalation of violence between Turkish military and militants of the Kurdish PKK claimed the lives of dozens of people every week during 2015. Upon entering Moda Sahnesi, I saw how the issue was addressed through the casting. My favourite character in the play, Nick Bottom, was played there by Caner Erdem in such a way that he resembled a working-class Kurdish citizen. His Kurdish accent and rebellious attitude towards the condescending Athenian elites were received with warm applause. He was the brightest character out there. I knew it. He knew it. And the audience knew it. Although both Yücel and Sabuncu had passed away, the rebellious spirit of the legendary Tepebaşı production was still alive. ⊗

Kaya Genç is a novelist, and a contributing editor to Index on Censorship magazine

ABOVE: Demetrius (Mert Firat) and Lysander (Onur Unsal) try to stop Hermia (Beyza Sekerci), who is enraged after Helena (Melis Birkan) mocks her height in Kemal Aydogan's A Midsummer Night's Dream

SPECIAL REPORT

Say no moor

45(01): 52/55 | DOI: 10.1177/0306422016643021

Dame Janet Suzman's staging of Othello squeezed past censors to cause uproar in apartheid South Africa. **Natasha Joseph** speaks to the actress and other South African experts about performing Shakespeare

RENOWNED ACTRESS AND director Dame Janet Suzman made her debut with the Royal Shakespeare Company 50 years ago in the Wars of the Roses. This amalgamation of four of William Shakespeare's plays into a trilogy remains, Suzman told Index on Censorship, as potent a political tale in 2016 as it was when she was a young actress. As this new year began, she saw resonance with the "power plays" unfolding in the British cabinet. And it was, of course, not the first time that Suzman had experienced the power of England's most famous playwright to transcend time and place with his gift for metaphor.

In 1987 she decided to stage Othello in her native South Africa, bringing "the moor of Venice" to life at Johannesburg's iconic Market Theatre. It was just two years since Prime Minister PW Botha had repealed one of apartheid's most reviled laws, the Immorality Act, which banned sexual relationships between people of different races. Even without the legislation, many white South Africans baulked at the idea of interracial desire. No wonder, then, that Suzman's production attracted what she has described as "millions of bags full of hate letters from people who thought that this was an outrage".

An erotically charged embrace between the white Venetian Desdemona and the black titular character, who was played by John Kani, drew the most horrified reactions. Suzman told the Open University in 2011: "Well, I tell you, there were lots of seats banging up the first night that happened at the Market Theatre, and people marching out and swearing and, you know, all that was going on. We thought yes, right on, that's it, we're touching a nerve here."

BOTTOM LEFT: Actors Albert Pretorius, Rob van Vuuren and James Cairns in the politically charged production The Three Little Pigs, written by Tara Notcutt and staged in Grahamstown, South Africa

BOTTOM RIGHT: Sonny Venkatrathnam asked his wife to send him a copy of Shakespeare's complete works while he was imprisoned on Robben Island in the 1970s. The book was passed around inmates, including Nelson Mandela, and became known as the Robben Island Bible

Nerves were touched, certainly, but in a country famous for sweeping censorship and restrictions on freedom of movement, speech and association, the play was not banned. Why? Because the apartheid government "would have been the laughing stock of the world if they had banned Shakespeare", Suzman told Index.

"Any government would be really embarrassed to ban Shakespeare," she said. "The apartheid government was frightened of ridicule. Everyone is frightened of laughter."

The government's rather scattershot, arbitrary approach to censorship also helped. The ruling National Party, Suzman said, stuck pretty much to the letter of the law – and Shakespeare was not mentioned by name in any legislation. So the show went on. It wasn't just the regime whose reaction had worried Suzman, though: before Othello began at the Market Theatre, she and Kani decided to approach the leaders of the then-banned African National Congress to ask for their permission to go ahead. "It was important for John to get the sanction of his brothers [to take part in a work by] this dead white man."

Three years later, the ANC was unbanned. In 1994 it became South Africa's first democratically elected and black-led government. Theatremakers no longer have to worry about their work being hauled to a censorship board that won't countenance any commentary on racism.

But Tara Notcutt, a playwright and director, said there has been a dearth of groundbreaking post-apartheid Shakespeare plays in recent years. Notcutt created the politically charged The Three Little Pigs, an allegorical examination of South African current affair, which premiered in 2012 at the National Arts Festival in Grahamstown in the country's south east. She told Index on Censorship that she feels Shakespeare and other established, more universal playwrights have taken a back seat to original, local theatre now that artists needn't actively fear the government. And what, in that outspoken and uncensored climate, is the state of South African protest theatre?

"I think the term 'protest theatre' is something which people associate with satire against a government, but I've found more recently that it can be more subtle than that," Notcutt said. "Something like Rob Murray's Waterline is a human look at the water shortage crisis in the Eastern Cape [province], which – yes – is protesting against the conditions, but I personally wouldn't call it protest theatre. It's more subtle, sophisticated and beautiful than my 1980s connection to →

ABOVE: Performers Joanna Weinberg, left, Richard Haines, centre, and John Kani, right, during a performance of Othello, directed by Janet Suzman at the Market Theatre in Johannesburg, in 1987

the term." Her play The Three Little Pigs, an examination of high levels of government corruption, drew "virtually no" condemnation or contempt from those in power.

Notcutt continued: "We got a lot of support for the things that we said in it, and I

Any government would be really embarrassed to ban Shakespeare. The apartheid government was frightened of ridicule

think that's because people generally agreed and felt the same way about what we said. But we're also really aware that the play was, for the most part, only seen by a certain group of people – that is, middle class, mostly white audiences. Different

ages, sure, but I'd go so far as to say that opinions that disagreed with what they saw were few and far between."

Chris Thurman, an associate English literature professor at the University of the Witwatersrand, believes there's another reason that Shakespeare doesn't feature strongly on the political theatre agenda.

"I think part of the reluctance is that previous attempts to use Shakespeare's plays as allegories for South African history or contemporary events have flopped," Thurman told Index on Censorship. "I'm thinking of the Market Theatre Titus Andronicus in 1995 and the Baxter Theatre 'African' Tempest in 2007. Yael Farber's SeZaR! [Julius Caesar] in 2000 was also a significant production, although one that, I think, buys into the essentialist, inaccurate sense that some plays 'fit' South Africa or some generic idea of Africa. These 'generic ideas' involve the themes of witchcraft,

BELOW: Fred Abrahamse's 2016 production of Othello at the Maynardville Open Air Theatre, Cape Town

Hiding Shakespeare on Robben Island

In Othello, "a black man is bullied by a white thug" – that's how Dame Janet Suzman describes it. But while bringing William Shakespeare's story to the stage during the apartheid era became feasible, finding a copy of the text proved much harder. Suzman told Index on Censorship she couldn't even pick up a written version of Othello from the local university bookshop, which she'd assumed would stock a wide range of literature.

One place she might have found it was the notorious prison on Robben Island. There, ANC and Pan African Congress leaders, such as Nelson Mandela, Robert Sobukwe, Walter Sisulu and Govan Mbeki, were imprisoned. Sonny Venkatrathnam was a prisoner on the island from 1972-78. During that time, authorities briefly relaxed the rules to allow inmates to have one book – other than a religious text – in their possession. As Venkatrathnam explained

decades later to British playwright Matthew Hahn, he cleverly asked his wife to send along a copy of Shakespeare's complete works. This, of course, contained far more than just one book.

The Robben Island Bible, as it became known, was passed around to many of Venkatrathnam's fellow inmates. It was confiscated at one point when the rules were changed arbitrarily again, but Venkathrathnam used religious greetings cards on the cover to disguise it as a holy book. Hahn explores the story in his play, the Robben Island Bible. The book made headlines after Mandela's death in December 2013 when it emerged that the global statesman had signed his name alongside this passage from Julius Caesar:

"Cowards die many times before their deaths;
The valiant never taste of death but once.
Of all the wonders that I yet have heard.
It seems to me most strange that men should fear;
Seeing that death, a necessary end,
Will come when it will come."

NJ

violent coups and the supernatural."

"It may be that over-determined allegorical uses of Shakespeare to deal with South African issues just don't work – they lack the nuance needed to tackle local complexities if you are too 'faithful' to the Shakespearean text as a template into which these things can't be forced," Thurman said.

As for Othello, the play recently had its second run in two years at Cape Town's 65-year-old Maynardville Open Air Theatre. If any seats banged up, they would have belonged to bored school children on a class trip. Does Suzman think Shakespeare remains relevant as a form of political commentary in a free society?

For her, the answer is an unequivocal "yes". Rewatching that 50-year-old

production of The Wars of the Roses made her think "no one has topped him for political playwriting".

"The wonder is that Shakespeare didn't get his head chopped off in his time. He kept his head down, below the parapet, by setting his plays in historical times. People pluck the present out of history." She said his writing also leaves itself "open to interpretation", making it "elastic" for directors who use his text to entertain or caution. "Shakespeare lends itself to anything," she said. "The glove fits any hand. You can tap lightly with it or punch hard." ⊗

Natasha Joseph is a contributing editor to Index on Censorship magazine, and is based in Cape Town, South Africa

GLOBAL VIEW

45(01): 56/57 | DOI: 10.1177/0306422016643022

Jodie Ginsberg on why silencing or no-platforming big names is not the way to win free speech battles, now or in the future

I AM NATURALLY ARGUMENTATIVE. I love a good debate – even (perhaps especially) the ones that make my blood boil. But, as I mark nearly two years at the helm of Index, it seems that, in the West at least, the spaces for debate are shrinking.

Student leaders are refusing to share platforms with those whose views they find offensive, governments are cranking up laws on speech in an effort to catch proto-extremists, and social-media mobs holler for pretty much everything, from Donald Trump to sombreros, to be banned.

The rise of identity politics, the conflation of offence with harm, technology's ability to enhance the power of the mob – all of these have been written about extensively in relation to such growing restrictions. But what gets less attention is the increasingly prevalent idea that underlies many of these attempts at censorship: the idea that silencing the "powerful" is the answer to a lack of voice for the minority.

At an event on free speech on campus organised by free-speech group Spiked! in February, I heard people argue that it is OK to prevent a well-known person from speaking because such individuals have plenty of avenues to speak elsewhere. They argued that preventing those high-profile characters

from talking simply starts to equal the balance between those who have platforms to speak and those who do not.

This does seem to be a growing position and one we should fight back against. Some of those arguing for the no-platforming of feminist author Germaine Greer at Cardiff University felt Greer already had too many opportunities to speak.

It's an alluring argument. But it is false. And it is false because it confuses failure of access with failures of speech. These two things have to be approached separately.

We also need to be clear that a lack of access to places on panels or at events for some groups in society means this market of ideas does not always work as effectively as it should.

All too often, in the debates about no-platforming speakers at universities, in the demands for writers to be prosecuted, in the attempts to get plays or figures banned, do we see people calling for censorship of the speech they don't like.

Censorship is never the answer for opinions you disagree with. Because as soon as you to start to undermine the idea that all speech is valid, then you lose the battle for your own voice to be heard.

In 2014, there was a furore over the cancellation of a show at the Barbican in London called Exhibit B. The work, by white South African artist Brett Bailey, used black actors to recreate the "human zoos" of the 19th century, which saw kidnapped Africans paraded as entertainment. Some 23,000 people signed a petition urging the Barbican to drop the show, which the venue eventually did following concerns about its ability to safely police protests outside.

Ahead of the cancellation, Index's associate arts producer Julia Farrington wrote an article looking at the role of institutions in managing controversial art and a lack of diversity in arts management in the

UK. Farrington wrote of "institutionalised mono-cultural bias" that was also a form of censorship.

Some of those who read the article after Exhibit B was cancelled interpreted this argument as one that in some way excused the cancellation of the piece. The decision to pull Exhibit B was censorship – pure and simple – but Farrington had a point. A lack of platform for diverse voices is a form of silencing.

And we should stop pretending that encouraging a diversity of viewpoints is somehow nanny-state tokenism. If you genuinely believe in free expression, then you should also believe in the importance of hearing other views, not just your own.

But the lack of platform for some must never be answered by removing the platform of others.

All too often ... in the attempts to get plays or figures banned, do we see people calling for censorship of the speech they don't like

There is another way. This year's Index on Censorship Freedom of Expression Awards shows how the world needs a range of people speaking out on different issues. From theatre producers working in a French refugee camp, to a female Syrian journalist who trains other women to tell their stories about the ongoing war, these extraordinary people work, day in day out, to give a voice to those who otherwise have limited access to platforms for speech. The megaphone, which is the motif for this year's awards, is an apt symbol for them all. ⊗

Jodie Ginsberg is the CEO of Index on Censorship. She tweets @jodieginsberg

OPPOSITE: A petition was launched in late 2015 to stop US presidential candidate Donald Trump from entering the UK after he said Muslims should be prevented from entering the USA. UK parliamentarians discussed the petition after it gained more than 500,000 signatures; Trump's views were widely condemned but most members agreed that banning him was not the answer

IN FOCUS

In this section

PICTURED: "Not forgetting, not forgiving" reads the text on a mural in the La Boca
neighbourhood of Buenos Aires, Argentina. It depicts a head-scarfed member of the Mothers
of Plaza, a group that protests for answers about the thousands of people who disappeared
during the country's military dictatorship

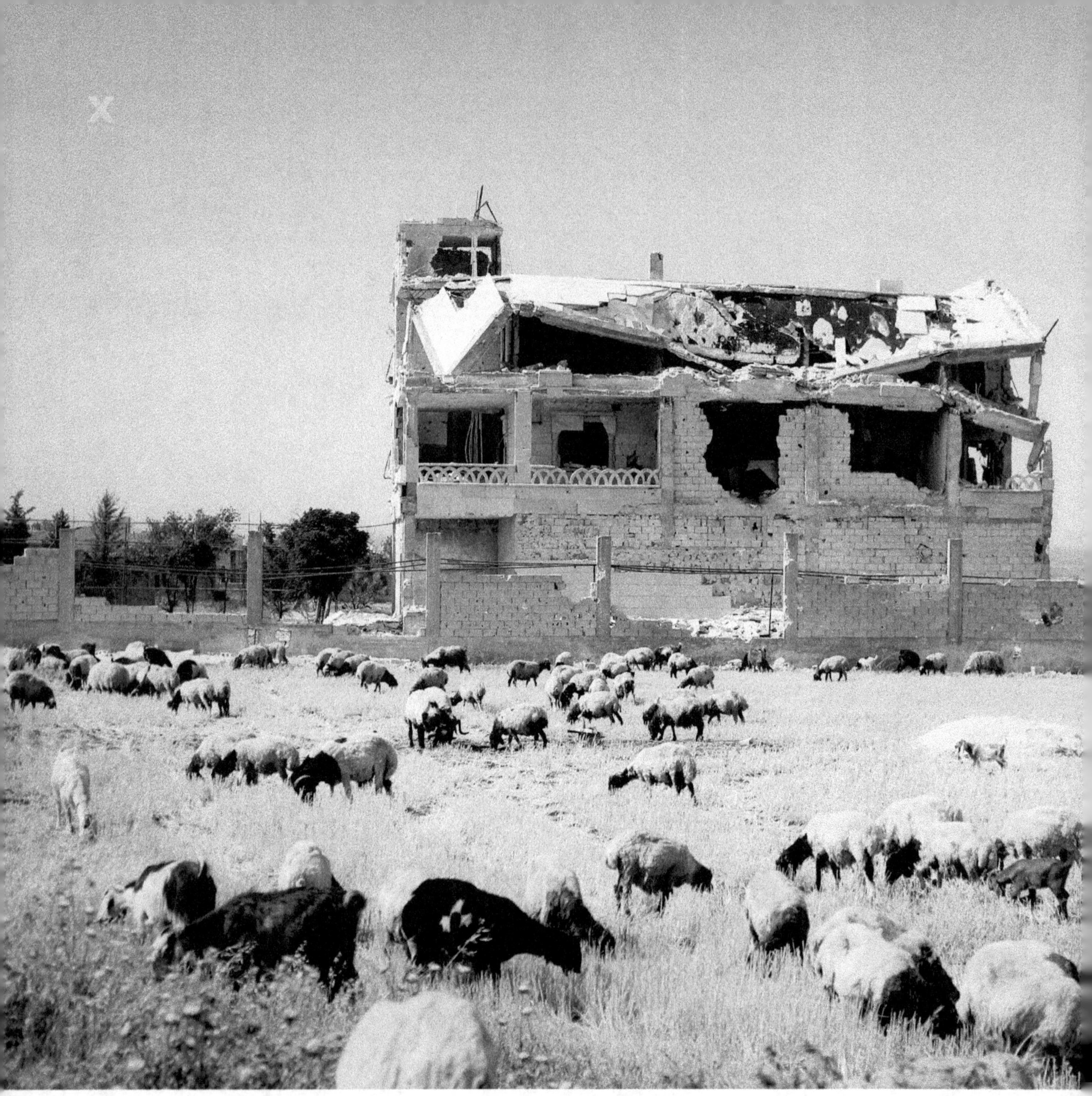

Credit: Reuters / Hamid Khatib

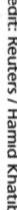

Theatre of war

45(01): 60/63 | DOI: 10.1177/0306422016643023

Syrian playwright **Liwaa Yazji** uses her play Goats to confront ideas that people are too afraid to talk about inside the war-torn country. **Charlotte Bailey** talks to her about finding more freedom in fiction

war. London's Royal Court Theatre has just finished presenting her writing as a work-in-progress at the Jerwood Theatre Downstairs; the theatre hopes that it will now tour extensively in the UK.

Goats covers an attempt to compensate families for their losses, with the local mayor offering a goat for each son martyred. As the town fills with goats, the community struggles to hold on to its sanity. "I became interested in following how surreal things can get," said Yazji, "How far they can go."

To research the play she travelled and met with people all over Syria. But Yazji, who grew up in Damascus and Aleppo, stressed that it is not a documentary. "The play does not copy-paste conversations," she said. The imaginative leap facilitated by fiction allows her to shed light on geographies and ideas

LEFT: Goats graze in front of a damaged building in the countryside around Aleppo, Syria. In Liwaa Yazji's play Goats the mayor of a Syrian town devises a compensation plan where families are given an animal for each son lost in the war

Damascus' once-thriving Opera House was badly damaged by a mortar attack in April 2014, but its doors remain open

"**A**M I REALLY harming my family? Will they be in trouble? Will they be investigated?" These are the questions that Syrian playwright Liwaa Yazji is asking herself about her latest work.

Working as a writer gets more complicated when your country is a war zone. There's pressure not to write, not to criticise, but there's so much to say. Yazji's latest play Goats tells the story of a small government-held town in Syria where families are struggling to cope with the impact of the civil

that can be hidden in traditional news media, she maintains. In pro-regime areas where she conducted her research, for instance, people did not want to speak out against the government. "If I said to people, tell me your situation, because I want to write [about] it, then it would be almost impossible [because people would be afraid]." So instead she worked to "understand the logic and the reasons they use to justify and answer certain complicated ethical questions, and then develop the discourse in the way that suits the text... in a play, you are free to imagine".

This imaginative piece represents a departure from her last project. In 2012 she directed the documentary Haunted, which explored what it means to flee home. Filming in Damascus was dangerous. The Syrian Network for Human Rights said in →

RIGHT: Syrian play-
wright Liwaa Yazji

Credits: (left) Ayham Deeb; (right) EPA/ Youssef Badawi

Liwaa Yazji

Yazji was born in Moscow in 1977, and
raised in Aleppo and Damascus in Syria.
Her first play Here in the Park was published in 2012, and her first poetry book
In Peace, We Leave Home in 2014. Her
documentary Haunted was released in
2014 and premiered in FID Marseilles
where it received a special mention in the
First Film Competition.

→ a June 2015 report that 22 artists have
been killed, and 57 have been arrested or
kidnapped since March 2011. The organisation also said reports of violence and crimes
against artists peaked in 2011 and 2012, but
numbers have since fallen, which they believe is because creative people are either less
active, have fled the country, or are keeping
quiet.

Her documentary focuses on people as they make the decision to leave their homes – what possessions they choose to take, what they choose to leave behind

The risks associated with Yazji's film were
even higher than with her play: she still fears
for the people remaining in Damascus who
were featured. "It is a really big responsibility," she said about using real people in her
film. "Whenever there is a screening I am
worried."

When the war first broke out she was
afraid of reprisals from the regime, but the
situation is now so chaotic and dangerous

that attacks could come from anywhere.
Yazji now spends most of her time between
Beirut and Berlin, where she is working on
a play about refugees, but she still travels
frequently to Syria – mostly to Damascus –
where her library remains.

After studying English literature at Damascus University, she graduated from
Syria's Higher Institute of Dramatic Art in
2003 and has been working in theatre in the
country ever since. Despite the war, there are
a two official theatres are still open in Damascus: the Higher Institute of Dramatic Art
and the Damascus Opera House, as well as a
few commercial theatres.

Damascus's once-thriving Opera House
was badly damaged by a mortar attack in
April 2014, but its doors remain open. At-
tendance even briefly swelled to pre-war
numbers in the December following the attack, according to Agence France Presse.
Yazji said, "A significant number [of people
still attend the theatre in Damascus] due to
the scarcity of social and cultural events and
the need to go to such events in bad times."

"Of course [people only go] if the security
situation permits," she added. "Needless to
say that there are new generations that are
growing in this war time and they also need

to live and practice social cultural life, since no limits of this war are seen in the near future."

The Wall Street Journal reported in August last year that the desire to keep the opera house open was "to convey a sense of business as usual".

Yazji sees herself as lucky that she was not banned from Syria for her film. Her understanding is that the "way the film was interpreted" meant she can still visit the city. Haunted focuses on people living in Damascus as they make the decision to leave their homes – what possessions they choose to take, what they choose to leave behind. While the context and the comments by the people in the film result in a piece critical of the regime, Yazji decided to "show this issue indirectly through the protagonists".

She said: "Political stands are there in the film if you wanted, as an audience, to follow hints and words, but the protagonists don't just stand in front of the camera cursing because this is not what the film is about." This was primarily an artistic choice, not a political one, she said.

She hopes the UK performances of Goats won't earn her a ban from re-entering her homeland, but the risk remains very real. She currently lives close to a circle of Syrian artists in Berlin; most have been exiled.

"I believe that a piece of art enlightens," she said. "It deserves to be read or to be seen, not banned. It might be useful even if you don't agree with me." ⊗

Charlotte Bailey is a journalist writing for newspapers including The Guardian. She was based in Beirut, Lebanon, working for the Daily Star, in 2015

BELOW: Musicians perform during the Arab Music Festival in the Damascus Opera House, also known as the Al Assad for Culture and Arts, in Damascus, Syria, in August 2015

Three priests on a remote island off the coast of Ireland managed to encapsulate Ireland's changing consciousness about the church and that delicate matter , that , the anointed ones might be as imperfect as the rest of us ; only funnier.

Credit: Kevin George / Alamy Stock Photo

Beyond belief

45(01): 64/67 | DOI: 10.1177/0306422016643024

At a time when many countries are phasing out blasphemy laws, in Ireland a similiar move is low on the political agenda. **Ryan McChrystal** asks whether the new government will finally take action

LET THE GO

Much of the conser
product of a no

church's influence in the affairs of independent Ireland. "In the name of God," it began. It was a marked break from that of 1867, in which the Irish Republican Brotherhood called for the "complete separation of church and state".

A hundred years on, many of the hangovers from the days of church influence on moral matters seem to be disappearing in Ireland. Same-sex marriage was legalised in 2015 following a nationwide referendum, and opposition to the anti-abortion laws is growing. But the campaign against the country's anachronistic blasphemy law has not yet picked up the same kind of momentum.

The government ruled out a referendum on the blasphemy law before this year's general election, which was brought forward suddenly to February. With the new shape of the government still being discussed as Index went to press, it was unclear what will be debated this year. Outgoing Taoiseach Enda Kenny agreed, back in January 2015, that a referendum was needed; the government had released a statement, three months prior, saying they first had to find an "appropriate

LEFT: Dublin artwork inspired by 1990s television comedy series Father Ted, which was about a group of dysfunctional priests., and which offended some Catholic viewers. In 2014, RTÉ, Ireland's public broadcaster, refused to show a comedy sketch, called Wild Nuns, which saw nuns oggling a semi-naked Jesus on the cross, as a parody of a Diet Coke advert

Ireland has the only blasphemy law introduced by a developed Western nation in the 21st century

IRELAND IS CURRENTLY engaging in nationwide self-reflection in commemoration of the 1916 Easter Rising, when republicans mounted an armed rebellion against British rule. Yet it is worth remembering that the insurgency was not just a catalyst for Irish independence, but also for the prominence of the Catholic church in Irish life ever since. This culminated in the passage of the controversial Defamation Act – the so-called blasphemy law – in 2009.

The Proclamation of 1916, issued at the beginning of the Rising, set the tone for the

date" to hold it.

Back in 1937, when the Irish Free State was declared, Éamon de Valera – Ireland's "founding father", and the only 1916 leader not executed by British forces – set about supervising the drafting of a new constitution. Significantly, it included a clause stating that "publication or utterance of blasphemous, seditious or indecent matter is an offence ... punishable in accordance with law".

Michael Nugent, chairperson of Atheist Ireland, has been campaigning for more attention to be paid to the blasphemy →

Acts of faith: blasphemy laws around the world

CANADA

Blasphemous libel (the crime of publishing blasphemous materials) is a criminal offence in Canada and perpetrators could face a prison sentence of up to two years, according to section 296 of Canada's 1982 Criminal Code. The government's last prosecution for blasphemous libel was in the 1930s, athough the law was invoked in private prosecutions as late as 1979.

ICELAND

Until last year blasphemy was a crime in Iceland, with a maximum penalty of three months in prison. The rescinding of the law in July 2015 was supported by the Church of Iceland, but opposed by others, including the Catholic Church of Iceland, and the Pentecostal Church.

NEW ZEALAND

Blasphemous libel is criminalised in New Zealand (section 123 of the Crimes Act 1961). The crime holds a maximum prison sentence of one year, although there are no successful prosecutions under this law on record, only one failed attempt in 1922. The act also states: "It is not an offence against this section to express in good faith and in decent language, or to attempt to establish by arguments used in good faith and conveyed in decent language, any opinion whatever on any religious subject."

PAKISTAN

Pakistan has one of the harshest blasphemy laws in the world, with prosecution carrying a possible death sentence (section 295 of the 1860 Penal Code). However, these laws could soon be reviewed as Muhammad Khan Sherani, chairman of a body that advises the government on the compatibility of laws with Islam, told Reuters in January 2016 he was willing to review the current penalties.

SAUDI ARABIA

In March 2014, the Saudi government furthered its harsh penalties for blasphemy, or apostasy – which already included a possible death sentence – by announcing new anti-terrorism legislation that defines atheism as terrorism. In May 2014, secular blogger Raif Badawi received a 10-year prison sentence, a fine of 1 million riyals (£175,000) and 1,000 lashes for insulting Islam and founding a liberal website; he has been detained since 2012.

Josie Timms

→ law and its origins. He told Index why the constitution lagged behind the times in modern Ireland: "The 1937 constitution was, and remains, a Catholic constitution, effectively co-written by de Valera and the future Catholic Archbishop of Dublin, John Charles McQuaid. It not only enshrines the right to worship a god, but also the right of that god to be worshipped."

The constitution's clause on blasphemy paved the way for the Defamation Act 1961, but it has proved ineffective. The only attempt to prosecute anyone under it came when the Irish Independent published a cartoon inspired by the 1995 divorce referendum, showing three politicians waving goodbye to a priest handing out the Eucharist. The prosecution was unsuccessful as the act failed to provide a clear definition of blasphemy. In effect, the offence of blasphemy, while included in the constitution, was not really enforceable by law.

It would take almost half a century for this ambiguity to be corrected – not by abolishing the offence (which would require a referendum), but by clarifying it. The Defamation Act 2009 defined blasphemous material as "grossly abusive or insulting in

relation to matters held sacred by any religion", when the intent and result is "outrage among a substantial number of the adherents of that religion". The offence still carries a maximum fine of €25,000 ($28,000).

The Defamation Act 2009 is the only blasphemy law introduced by a Western nation in the 21st century. But using blasphemy laws is not going out of style. Russia passed a similar law in 2013, which allows for up to three years' imprisonment (Mission Creep, vol 42.04, p36), meanwhile reports from Croatia and Poland show (Fired, Threatened and Imprisoned, vol 44.02, p70) the rising influence of the church to influence government policy. The Irish law was implemented in spite of the Law Reform Commission's opinion that "there is no place for the offence of blasphemous libel in a society which respects freedom of speech". Even Dermot Ahern, the minister for justice who passed the law, described blasphemy as an "arcane concept". So why introduce the act at all?

"The thinking seems to have been that it was unsatisfactory to have a provision of the constitution voided by legislative omission – which seems, from a strict rule of law perspective, to have some foundation," said Eoin Carolan, a senior lecturer at University College Dublin and an expert in Irish constitutional law. "What was more curious was that the then government did not take the alternative option of seeking to remove the provision from the constitution by referendum, the justification being that a referendum would be too expensive."

Nugent had another theory on the lack of action: "We're so immunised to how ridiculous and silly the blasphemy law is that it doesn't have the same effect on people as, say, the abortion issue." Not that this has stopped Atheist Ireland from trying. In 2010, it established a campaign to challenge the law and tested it by publishing statements blaspheming all major religions. "If we had been prosecuted, we would have challenged the constitutionality of the act. But as we

haven't been so far, we argue that this undermines its credibility," said Nugent.

Among Christians, belief in the law's effectiveness appears to be waning, even if this has yet to translate into a concerted campaign to repeal it. At a Constitutional Convention in 2013, the Irish Council of Churches – speaking for all major Christian denominations in the country – declared that the constitutional ban on blasphemy is

The Organisation of Islamic States at the UN, led by Pakistan, now cites Ireland's law as best practice

"largely obsolete". "Most Irish Catholics don't really think of religion anymore, except when it comes to rituals like weddings and funerals," Arthur Mathews, co-writer of TV series Father Ted, told Index on Censorship. "As the Irish have largely moved into a liberal interpretation of religion, they are open to occasionally being the subject of satire."

And yet, even as the Defamation Act is failing to inspire widespread protest among the Irish, it is setting an example for others abroad. The Organisation of Islamic States at the UN now cites Ireland's law as best practice. The OIS is led by Pakistan, a country where Asia Bibi, a Christian woman, is awaiting execution for having drunk the same water as her Muslim neighbours and insulted the Prophet.

A law which punishes anything that causes "outrage" is all too open to abuse. If anything should shake the people of Ireland out of their complacency on this issue, it is examples of such abuse, whether at home or abroad. Just ignoring a law because no one is using it right now means you are forgetting that, one day, someone might.

Ryan McChrystal is online assistant editor for Index on Censorship

Exposing history's faultlines

45(01): 68/71 | DOI: 10.1177/0306422016643025

On the 40th anniversary of the Argentinian coup that led to the disappearance of around 30,000 people, **Vicky Baker** interviews those who were imprisoned, threatened or lost family

"**ON 15 MAY** Susana Martínez, a 29-year-old teacher and writer of poems and children's stories, disappeared from the house of her friend who was looking after her one-year-old baby." This was in 1977. Martínez never returned home. As the 40th anniversary of her disappearance approaches, a plaque bearing her name has been recently placed in a public square, Plaza Primero de Mayo, in central Buenos Aires.

That short sentence, announcing a woman's disappearance in unknown circumstances, is taken from a 1977 issue of Index on Censorship magazine. There were no further details. It is unlikely anybody had further details to give. The entry was part of a regular feature that was integral to this magazine's early years. At the end of each issue, the Index Index listed violations of free expression taking place around the world, from magazine closures and threats of violence, to imprisonments and murders. Arranged alphabetically, under subheadings for individual countries, it ran from the magazine's

inception in 1972 until 2012.

Cristina and Richard Whitecross were also listed in the Index Index. The couple were under surveillance for hosting political refugees who had fled after General Augusto Pinochet's coup in neighbouring Chile. One of their guests, the dean of the University of Santiago, was arrested with them. "He survived," Cristina Whitecross told Index on the phone from her home in Oxford this year, "but I was made to watch while he was being tortured." Whitecross said she was never physically tortured herself, but Richard was beaten on various occasions and they feared for their lives throughout.

Reading the entries for Argentina during its dictatorship years shows the frightening pace that the military junta's grip on power strengthened and censorship restrictions became tighter than ever. After overthrowing President Isabel Peron on 24 March 1976, they launched a brutal regime, which led to approximately 30,000 people being "disappeared". The junta was brought down at the end of 1983, and more details gradually came to light about their clandestine torture centres, the bodies thrown from planes into the River Plate, and the stolen babies, many of whom have families still searching for them today.

The collated entries from Argentina in the Index Index during this era run to 14,000 words and hundreds of individual stories. The story of Cristina Whitecross (née Lange) and her husband, Richard, features in a 1976 issue: "Cristina Elvira Lange, a lecturer in linguistics, together with her English-born husband, Richard Whitecross, a commercial representative of several British publishing companies, were arrested by the security forces on 24 November [1975] on charges of contacts with guerrilla groups and have since been detained without trial under the country's 'state of siege' in the Villa Devoto prison in Buenos Aires."

To this day, Whitecross believes they were saved by a couple of fortunate occurrences,

including a disruption at a military news conference not long after they were arrested. "General Videla [the leader of the regime] held a press conference to tell the world they were good guys," she said. "They invited lots of foreign journalists and our personal friend, Stuart Russell from Reuters, was

It was forbidden to report, comment or make reference to the appearance of bodies and the deaths

there. Of course, you had to hand in your questions beforehand, and after Stuart had asked his, he continued. He said to Videla, 'I can't report favourably on the coup while you have Cristina and Richard Whitecross and no one knows where they are.' It was a huge scandal and it was pretty daring of him because journalists disappeared too. It was also extremely important for us because immediately after that we appeared [as registered prisoners] in Villa Devoto prison. In other words, they had to recognise that we were somewhere. Before that, you were held in a sort of limbo and that was dangerous."

They were finally released after 138 days and moved to the UK, where they built lives working as publishers and human rights campaigners. They had two sons, one of whom is an actor and teacher, the other is a filmmaker who, inspired by his parents' experiences, co-directed the documentary Road to Guantanamo with Michael Winterbottom.

Reading the Index Index chronologically, issue by issue, the unfolding horror story is as frightening as it is indiscriminate. The early issues, even before the junta took power, show the early crackdown on left-wing magazines, but soon an extreme paranoia saw everyone from language teachers to whole families of psychologists appearing on the lists. There's also poignancy in the →

OPPOSITE: Members of the human rights group Madres de Plaza de Mayo (mothers of the disappeared) on the 30th anniversary of the 1976 military coup (March 24, 2006)

ABOVE: Cristina White-cross with her husband Richard after they were released from prison in Argentina

remember my father always seemed very present. Then, as I grew up, it became clearer, and I began to access information for myself, asking not just what happened to my father, but also who was my father." It's a story he is now trying to pass on to his own young son.

Such is Conti's legacy that in 2008, part of the Esma military school, which was used by the junta as a torture centre and has since been reclaimed as a museum, became the Haroldo Conti Cultural Centre.

The Buenos Aires Herald, an English-language newspaper, bravely decided to report on Conti's disappearance at the time. Andrew Graham-Yooll, an Anglo-Argentine journalist who worked for the paper at the time and later became editor of Index on Censorship, still remembers the day he found out the news at a lunch meeting. "I had friends of Conti telling me I had to publish and there was a naval officer who said 'Don't you dare, you know what will happen to you.' I left without saying anything." He published straight away, but admits everyone was terrified.

The previous mouth, April 1976, the Buenos Aires Herald had also courageously confronted the junta's ban on mentioning the disappeared by publishing extracts of a ruling that officials passed to the press on small slips of paper, without a letterhead or signature. It reported: "From April 22 it is forbidden to report, comment or make reference to subjects related to subversive incidents, the appearance of bodies and the deaths of subversive elements and/or members of the armed or security forces, unless these are announced by a responsible official source. This includes kidnappings and disappearances."

While they were locked up, prisoners had their own techniques for trying to share information with the world. Those inside Villa Devoto prison often shouted out names in unison, hoping that their voices would be heard above the walls and in the surrounding neighbourhood. Those that were freed desperately tried to memorise information about

→ reports' brevity; those we know survived are listed next to those that didn't.

Haroldo Conti, a writer and teacher, never returned to his home after armed men raided it in May 1976. His case remains one of the most famous from the era. Index on Censorship published news of his disappearance in September 1976, after information had been fed back to London. Later in 1981, the magazine also carried an article by Gabriel García Márquez titled The Last and Bad News of Haroldo Conti. Describing the lead up to the disappearance, Márquez wrote: "In February 1976, Martha [Conti's wife] gave birth to a boy, whom they named Ernesto. From then on, Haroldo Conti hung a notice opposite his desk: 'This is my place of combat, and from here I'll not move'. But his kidnappers never knew what the notice said, because it was written in Latin."

Ernesto Conti, now in his forties and working in political communications, spoke to Index from Buenos Aires. "I was tiny when my father was kidnapped. We went into exile with my mother and I spent my first 10 years outside of the country," he said. "From when I was very young, my mother tried to unfold all that had happened, while taking into account that I was still a child. I

their fellow captives, so they could pass on messages and news of their whereabouts.

Graham-Yooll regularly fed information about the disappearances to Index on Censorship and Amnesty International, before being forced into exile with his family. "I'd send it via airmail, but never too thick and never anything as ostentatious as an airmail envelope. I also used to send old-fashion telegrams to Amnesty via the Daily Telegraph, as a cover-up." Graham-Yooll left the country after the Buenos Aires Herald was raided,

but returned to Argentina.

Reading through the Index Index, it is easy to assume those who were released and left Argentina were then free from surveillance, but Whitecross said it was not that simple. She remembered a visit to her Oxford home from a suspicious man, posing as a gas technician. "When I called the gas board, they said they hadn't sent anyone and they didn't work on Saturdays, which is when he said he'd come back. To this day, I don't know if this was related, but we knew from [what happened in] South Africa that groups get infiltrated. In Argentina's case, they used people from the navy. And there were cases of people being followed, so it felt perfectly possible."

Those inside Villa Devoto prison often shouted out names in unison, hoping that their voices would be heard above the walls and in the surrounding neighbourhood

Richard Whitecross died in 2009 after suffering from Alzheimer's disease. "At one point he had a flashback and thought we were back in prison and he was telling me to be careful. It was heartbreaking, but then he was back to his normal, lovely self."

Cristina Whitecross remains as defiant today as she was at the time. As they boarded the plane after being released, she remembers being questioned by a police officer. "He asked if I was being released thanks to General Videla. And I said, 'Can I rephrase that and say I am being released in spite of General Videla?'." ⊗

Vicky Baker is deputy editor of Index on Censorship magazine. She tweets at @vickybaker. Additional research of Index archives by Jon Wilcox

---

Argentina's Dirty War

24 MARCH 1976
A military coup d'état, under General Jorge Videla, overthrows President Isabel Perón

22 APRIL 1976
Memo passed on to press, forbidding them to mention kidnappings and disappearances

22 DECEMBER 1981
General Leopoldo Galtieri takes over as leader of the military regime

2 APRIL 1982
War against Britain over the Falkland Islands breaks out in the South Atlantic, and lasts for two months

10 DECEMBER 1983
Argentina returns to civilian rule as President Raúl Alfonsín assumes power

Rainbow warriors

45(01): 72/75 | DOI: 10.1177/0306422016643026

Gay activists in Honduras are facing torture, prison and assassination.
Duncan Tucker reports on the largely uninvestigated killings that are
slipping under the radar of the rest of the world

A YEAR AFTER RETURNING from exile, Honduran gay rights activist Donny Reyes still fears a murderous attack at any minute.

"I've been imprisoned on many occasions. I've suffered torture and sexual violence because of my activism, and I've survived many assassination attempts," he said, in an interview with Index on Censorship.

Activists in Honduras must contend with a constant barrage of threats and, often fatal, attacks. Reyes, the coordinator of the Honduran lesbian, gay, bisexual, and transgender advocacy group Arcoíris (Rainbow), had spent 10 months abroad for his own safety, but felt an obligation to return to the frontline of the fight against discrimination.

"To be able to continue with my personal life and my work I have to be conscious that [death] could come at any moment," he said. "The truth is it doesn't worry me anymore. What worries me is that things won't change."

Dozens of LGBT Hondurans are murdered each year, with few of the killers brought to justice, according to figures from respected Honduran NGO Cattrachas. Journalists and activists who speak out are often attacked. One of these was Juan Carlos Cruz Andara who died after being stabbed 25 times by unknown assailants last June.

Arcoíris reported 15 security incidents against its members during the second half of 2015, including surveillance, harassment, arbitrary detentions, assaults, robberies, theft, threats, sexual assault and even murder. Other LGBT activists have experienced forced evictions, fraudulent charges, defamation, enforced disappearances and restrictions of right to assembly.

The activists consulted by Index all said that the level of homophobic violence exploded after the ousting of liberal President Manuel Zelaya in the military coup of 2009. The election of right-wing candidate Porfirio Lobo Sosa the following year coincided with the militarisation of Honduras, a rise in gang-related violence, and a clampdown on human rights.

The records from Cattrachas show that on average two LGBT people were murdered each year in the country from 1994 to 2008. After the 2009 coup that rate rocketed to an average 31 murders per year, according to figures from Arcoíris. In early 2016 there were signs the situation was escalating further with the murder of Paola Barraza, a member of Arcoiris's group, on 24 January. In reality though it is impossible to know precisely how many people have been killed because of their sexuality because the vast majority of cases remain unsolved.

Erick Martínez Salgado, who volunteers with LGBT advocacy group Kukulcanhn, told Index that gay activists protested heavily against discrimination and the coup.

215 [1]

LGBT people murdered in Honduras between 2009 and 2015

HOMOPHOBIA IN HONDURAS

37

deaths in 2015 alone

San Pedro Sula was the world's most violent city in 2014, with **171.2** murders per 100,000 inhabitants. [3]

From 1994 to 2008 an average of **2** LGBT people were murdered each year in Honduras. [2] An average of **31** LGBT people per year have been killed between the 2009 coup and the end of 2015.

Of the **235** murders of LGBT people since 1994, only **48** cases (20%) have gone to court. [4]

27 trans women were assassinated in Honduras between 2009 and 2012. [5]

Since the 2009 coup, murder rates in Honduras have soared, with LGBT people under specific threat. It is impossible to know precisely how many people have been killed because of their sexuality as most cases are never investigated.

Sources: 1, 2, 4 cattrachas.org; 3 seguridadjusticiaypaz.org.mx; 5 redlactrans.org.ar

By Ryan McChrystal

Continuaremos Exigiendo Justicia

ABOVE: Friends of Honduran gay rights activist Walter Tróchez, who was killed in a drive-by shooting, stage a candlelight vigil to mark the third anniversary of his death in Tegucigalpa, December 2012

→ He believes the government came to view his group as a threat to the traditional social order and started targeting them to "send a message" to other protesters.

One of the most prominent gay rights activists of the time, Walter Tróchez, was killed in a drive-by shooting in December 2009. Human rights groups noted that he had previously been kidnapped, beaten and threatened for demonstrating against the coup and advocating for gay rights. Four years later, Tróchez's friend and fellow gay rights activist Germán Mendoza was arrested and charged with his murder.

Mendoza told Index he was held in deplorable conditions and repeatedly tortured in a bid to make him plead guilty. Eventually he was released after proving his innocence

last year. Mendoza believes he was arrested because the government wanted to use him "as a scapegoat to wash their hands of the responsibility" for Tróchez's death, which remains unsolved. The Honduran government did not respond to requests for comment.

Gang warfare was a massive contributor to Honduras status as the nation with the world's highest murder rate in 2012, however the gay community's main concern is not gangs, but the state security forces.

"The police constitute the primary perpetrator of violations of the rights of the LGBT community," the Coalition Against Impunity, an alliance of 29 Honduran NGOs, warned last year, citing alleged "police policy of frequent threats, arbitrary arrests, harassment, sexual abuse, discrimination, torture and

cruel or degrading treatment".

As a result many vulnerable activists are reluctant to ask for protection, for fear that contact with the police would expose them to greater security risks or reprisals.

The journalists who document homophobic violence in Honduras also risk their lives. Dina Meza, an independent investigative reporter who has covered the issue extensively, was nominated for an Index on Censorship Freedom of Expression Award in 2014 for her journalism. Meza said the country's mainstream media often portrays the LGBT community in a negative light.

Meza, who launched the independent news site Pasos de Animal Grande last year to draw attention to the hardships facing the most vulnerable sectors of society, said reporters who cover violence against the LGBT community are also targeted. She said not only do journalists get physically assaulted by the security forces and expelled from public events, but they are also targets of government-led smear campaigns.

"It's extremely common here for them to link human rights defenders to drug trafficking and organised crime, in a bid to sow doubts in people's minds about the work that we're doing," she explained. "If we speak out at an international level they say we're trying to undermine Honduras, discourage investment and see the country burn."

Peter Tatchell, director of the London-based LGBT campaigning group the Peter Tatchell Foundation, called for the world to pay more attention to the killings. He said: "This extensive, shocking mob violence against LGBT Hondurans is almost unreported in the rest of the world. The big international LGBT organisations tend to focus on better-known homophobic repression in countries like Egypt, Russia, Iran and Uganda. What's happening in Honduras is many times worse. Is this neglect because it is a tiny country with few resources and no geo-political weight? The UN, Organisation of American States and foreign aid providers need to do more to press the Honduran government to crackdown on anti-LGBT hate crime and to educate the public on LGBT issues to combat prejudice."

Meza and the activists interviewed by Index also believe that Catholic and Evangelical Christian groups have become increasingly influential in Honduran society. Reyes from Arcoíris described the state, the church and the mainstream media as a triumvirate which has fuelled "impunity, fundamentalism, machismo and misogyny" across the country, with disastrous consequences for the LGBT community.

"At home and at school are the first two places where we're attacked and discriminated. We flee home at very young ages because the family is built on religious values. Our

We can be sex workers or street vendors or stay in the closet, but if they find out about your sexual orientation you'll almost certainly be fired

families punish us in a cruel manner and this has a terrible psychological impact," Reyes said. "Our educational and employment opportunities are diminished every day. We can be sex workers or street vendors, or stay in the closet in the hope of getting a job, but if they find out about your sexual orientation you'll almost certainly be fired."

Despite the risks he and his fellow activists face, Reyes said the drastic need for change is what gives them the strength to keep fighting discrimination: "We need a Honduras that's free from violence and homophobia. We believe it's our responsibility to fight for this so the next generation have a space to live in a better world." ⊗

Duncan Tucker is a journalist based in Mexico, who writes regularly for Index on Censorship

Hack job

45(01): 76/79 | DOI: 10.1177/0306422016643027

New Zealander **Frank Feinstein** has spent years archiving and hacking North Korea's news to help expose what's really happening inside this secretive regime. **Sybil Jones** interviews him to find out why, and how

"**THERE TOOK PLACE** a world-startling event to be specially recorded in the national history spanning 5,000 years." This is how the Korean Central News Agency, North Korea's official mouthpiece, broke the news of their supposed hydrogen bomb testing in January.

It showed the typically hyperbolic, nationalist style of news reporting that is behind all of North Korea's other online news and propaganda outlets. And it shows why independent news coverage on North Korea is so badly needed.

For nearly four years New Zealander Frank Feinstein has been monitoring KCNA through the service KCNA Watch (kcnawatch.nknews.org), part of an independent North Korea-focused news site. Feinstein told Index that although North Korea is still one of the most oppressive states in the world, the internet age means "its mechanisms of control leave a trail behind". KCNA Watch was established to follow those trails.

The service monitors North Korea's official news for the movements of the country's rulers, as well as looking at the stories they like and promote. It's also an open-source archive for stories that were once showing in Pyongyang's KCNA-dominated news sites, but have now disappeared. It's needed because KCNA re-edits and deletes stories that it doesn't like, just as George Orwell's Ministry of Truth did in his novel 1984. It even tries to stop search engines finding them, using a design that prevents external archiving, successfully frustrating even Google. For example, a reader could take a current news headline or text from KCNA's site (kcna.kp), put it into Google's search engine and follow the offered links. But nothing will come up.

Yet sometimes all the North Korean government's attempts to rub out public

information fail. Feinstein's biggest scoop came in December 2013, following Pyongyang's swift and public purging of Jang Song Thaek, Kim Jong Un's uncle and previously one of North Korea's most powerful men. Jang was executed after being accused of being a traitor.

Hundreds of articles mentioning Jang rapidly disappeared, and the targeted erasing of one man's history soon escalated into the mass deletion of all 39,000 articles which had appeared before October 2013. It was a wipe-out across North Korea's online news sites that, to Pyongyang's annoyance,

Feinstein recorded and reported. At the time he told Index on Censorship that it was "the largest 'management' of its online archive North Korea has engaged in since it went online".

But there were consequences for bringing this to the world's attention. Feinstein believes that Pyongyang took revenge against his archiving and "banned the entirety of New Zealand" from accessing North Korea's servers. Feinstein has accounts with the four sites that have New Zealand's largest range of internet protocol addresses. These identify particular computers and routers and →

ABOVE: A poster for The Interview, a US comedy about an imagined assassination plot against North Korean leader Kim Jong-un, on the streets of New York City. The FBI blamed North Korea for the cyber attack against Hollywood studio Sony Pictures in December 2014

their geographical location – information that others can trace and use to block them. When he noticed there was a blockage, Feinstein said: "I tested each individually, then rang my internet service provider to test the maximum ranges they had available for North Korea. All came back banned." Feinstein, who has a doctorate in computer science, then asked his contacts in New Zealand's IT field to test their IP ranges, and, along with the main telecommunications firms, they confirmed their ranges were banned. But it was not universal. Frank said contacts in Australia "unanimously confirmed that every Australian address was able to access North Korean sites, but New Zealand IPs were blocked."

However, there are those who fight back. Feinstein said numerous people have claimed to have hacked North Korea's intranet (called Kwangmyong), a system designed to monitor individual users across the country.

"Hacking is getting you somewhere that the target system didn't intend," he said, adding, it's often "script kiddies" who hack North Korea when it's in fashion. As NK News' chief technical officer, he said: "It would sometimes fall in my position to

The targeted erasing of one man's history soon escalated into the mass deletion of all 39,000 articles

verify these claims from people outside the 'professional sphere'. I'd follow these up – not independently – but to 'prove' that it can be done." Hence he is a hacker, but not the destructive kind.

Far from the stereotypical bedroom-locked, Red Bull-fuelled script kiddy, Feinstein is the professional, urbane, 35-year-old director of a data-archiving company, Feinstein Doak, which tracks and archives social media and online publications, mainly of people or institutions in power and

authority. He said: "If you're a public figure in New Zealand and make a silly Facebook post, then delete it, nonetheless it's probably been permanently archived already by me."

Feinstein first became interested in censorship and propaganda years ago when he lived in Lithuania; his wife's Soviet-era school textbooks fascinated him in the way they deleted public figures as they fell out of political favour. He came to learn basic Korean from his older brother, who was living in South Korea, then over years he taught himself to read and write the language, as he became intrigued by North Korea's own news output. It was when an injury sidelined him from work that he had the time, skills and curiosity to set up KCNA Watch.

And it's clear that his work has been spotted by the North Korean authorities. "They do view me as a threat," he told Index, adding that there is "probably someone in North Korea in charge of stopping me, [… but] there's nothing they can do about it." He said that technical assistance from China has improved North Korea's security systems to cover its estimated three servers, 1,300 IP addresses and 550 URLs as of 2014, but "they still can't beat me".

His opponents across the keyboards are well-funded and have plenty of resources. According to professor Kim Heung-Kwang, who taught computer science at North Korea's Hamheung Computer Technology University before defecting in 2004, North Korea has a 6,000-strong corps of cyber-warfare specialists, and regularly targets South Korea's government and corporate IT infrastructure. Feinstein said: "North Korea is a viable and real cyber security threat to numerous Western countries, but specifically the USA."

North Korea's most famous alleged assault was in November 2014 when Sony Pictures Entertainment's systems suffered a malware shutdown and several terabytes of data were hacked. A group called Guardians of Peace claimed it was behind the attack,

but North Korea was put in the frame by the Guardians' demand that Sony cancel the imminent release of the comedy film The Interview, which notoriously features an assassination plot against Kim Jong-Un. Within weeks the FBI announced it had proof linking North Korea to the hack, saying North Korean IP addresses were associated with the malware, and malicious software was of North Korean origin. These accusations led to more sanctions being applied against the already isolated country. But while Pyongyang condoned the attack, it denied involvement. Several Western IT analysts, including Wired.com's Kim Zetter, Defcon organiser and CloudFlare researcher Marc Rogers, and Kurt Stammberger from cyber security firm Norse, said the FBI's case was flimsy.

Still, based on off-the-record evidence, Feinstein is convinced North Korea was involved. Proof is difficult to quantify, he said: "No one is ever going to spill the beans on this. No one can go on record without implicating other individuals that have gained trust."

It's worth remembering hackers come in all forms and they work for all sides. Days after the USA accused Pyongyang over Sony, North Korea's sole connection to the internet was knocked offline, which some blamed on the CIA. The speed with which the USA affirmed North Korea's guilt supported ideas that the National Security Agency had long been accessing North Korea's computer networks via secret access points used by South Korean intelligence – and had done so without South Korea's knowledge.

All sides use news as a weapon. The long-awaited effort to direct BBC World Service broadcasts at North Korea was announced in the UK government's 2015 national security strategy. Feinstein said: "America and the UK care far more about North Korea than many South Koreans do", and their media is dominated by publications reflecting their national interest. Nonetheless, even with the Chomskian model of "manufactured

consent", he believes comparisons between the West and totalitarian models are invalid.

The West's bias and propaganda is "much more sophisticated" than the "blunt" propaganda from both North Korea and South Korea. "South Korea is a straight-out authoritarian state with regards to media. In fact, it's simply illegal to print anything from North Korea in the South, and that's why

There is probably someone in North Korea in charge of stopping me; there's nothing they can do about it

I'm banned there," he said. Just weeks before the purging of news about Jang Song Thaek in North Korea, South Korea blocked KCNA Watch under the arcane 1948 National Security Act, which prohibits any published material of Pyongyang origin. "You have better access from Tuvalu to North Korea than you do in South Korea," said Feinstein.

Feinstein has been invited to North Korea – by whom he will not say – but has declined because he worried it could put his brother, who still lives in South Korea, in a difficult situation. Now after four years spent monitoring North Korea, Feinstein has decided to swap technology and hacking, to re-train in medicine. "In my training in medicine, it'd be very easy to diagnose both the North and South as paranoid schizophrenics," he said. He added that it seemed the overall thirst for propaganda outweighed any substantial demand for real news about North Korea. Hence in part why Feinstein is changing careers as he seeks to start a family. "I utterly do not want to be doing this sort of hacking work when that happens," he said. ⊗

Sybil Jones is a pseudonym. The writer regularly visits North Korea. NK News is an independent, privately owned specialist information source that focuses on North Korea (nknews.org)

"They worried I'm dangerous? I'm absolutely harmless"

45(01): 80/82 | DOI: 10.1177/0306422016643028

When academic **Steven Salaita** was fired from a US university for outspoken comments on Twitter, he brought debates about academic freedom into the headlines. **Nan Levinson** interviews him about the challenges to free speech in the classroom

STEVEN SALAITA, A professor of indigenous studies, opened his email at the beginning of August 2014 to find that the academic appointment at the University of Illinois at Urbana-Champaign that he was about to assume had evaporated. When the administration explained that the decision came in response to his activity on Twitter, where he was vividly criticising Israel's military action in Gaza, his firing quickly became a cause célèbre among US academics, who saw it as a direct challenge to academic freedom and another step toward constricting and sanitising university life. The following months were, Salaita said recently, "a whirlwind". Only now is he able to reflect on the larger issues.

In public statements, the university maintained that it took issue with the tone, not the content, of the tweets, that the problem was Salaita's lack of civility, but he thought otherwise. Charging breach of contract and violation of his free speech rights, he sued the university the following January. Index reported on the case in Stifling Freedom, (vol. 44, 2: pp. 20-25).

After being jobless for that turbulent year, Salaita currently holds the Edward W. Said Chair of American Studies at the American University of Beirut. He was still bemused by the tumult as he spoke with Index. "Now, being back at work, I go to department meetings, I go to lunch with my colleagues, I teach class, grade papers, I think, man, they were worried I am dangerous? I'm absolutely harmless."

In reaction to Salaita's firing, scholars boycotted the university and the American Association of University Professors voted to censure the university. In August after a court upheld Salaita's lawsuit, the chancellor and the university's top administrator resigned.

Finally last November the legal case was settled with a reported $600,000 payout. Although Salaita relinquished any claim to his promised job, he said, in a prepared statement. "This settlement is a vindication for me, but more importantly, it is a victory for academic freedom and the First Amendment."

While the final resolution may come this June, when the AAUP revisits its previous

censure decision, this argument, like many over what can and cannot be said, was a stand-in for a deeper tension, namely the relationship between what teachers profess as private citizens and what they teach in the classroom.

Salaita, an American of Jordanian and Palestinian heritage and an organiser of the Academic and Cultural Boycott of Israel, finds the teaching and attitude towards academic freedom at AUB similar to that at the US universities on which it's modelled. "Once inside the classroom the same set of dynamics prevail," he said.

In his classroom, the dynamics include political discussions, but he explicitly urges his students to work out and defend their own ideas, rather than ascribe to a particular point of view. Still he likes to mix it up.

"One thing I bring into the classroom is a desire to have interesting debate. I think students can handle rigorous discussion. In fact, I think they enjoy it and find it very useful. So in my classes, we tend to have something of a freewheeling set of discussions," he said with a wry laugh. "But we always come in on friendly terms and leave on friendly terms."

In response to Salaita's firing, then UIUC Chancellor Phyllis Wise sent a mass mailing to the campus community called Principles on Which We Stand. She wrote that while debate is important, a classroom needs to be a safe space (which Salaita would not contest). She implied that his tweets would translate into intimidation and harassment of students holding opposing opinions. That, he argues, is nonsense; despite efforts to →

ABOVE: Protesters at the University of Illinois at Urbana-Champaign campaign against the firing of professor Steven Salaita. Academics also voted to censure the university. The university's chancellor, Phyllis Wise, sent a mass mail to students, defending the decision and saying classrooms need to be safe spaces

find evidence to the contrary, reviews of his teaching are said to be stellar.

What constitutes a safe space, however, is more complex than positive student evaluations. A classroom, as every student knows, is not a democracy, and even if a teacher doesn't state his or her politics explicitly, they can usually be intuited. Students, in thrall to authority or out of eagerness to please or fear of reprisal, may feel pressured to agree

I think students can handle rigorous discussion. In fact, I think they enjoy it

or keep silent. So a professor's speech inside and outside the classroom is probably never clearly separated. What is different now is that external speech acts are readily available for everyone to see and react to through social media.

Laura Markwardt, media and communication strategist for AAUP, wrote in an email, "In recent years we have found that faculty members are more frequently finding themselves in trouble for extra-mural speech disseminated on the internet, especially in social media." This was Salaita's fate. He continues to be a busy user of Twitter and finds it a liberating, but not trouble-free platform, given that passions of the moment are recorded there in perpetuity.

His tweets, he agrees, were intemperate and angry, as his detractors charged, because they reflected how he was feeling at the time. "How are we supposed to act in the face of injustice?" he asked. "Sometimes we need to articulate a sense of political anger in relation to injustice, and particularly in cases where we're either directly or indirectly implicated."

Still, Salaita has no difficulty distinguishing what he tweets from how he teaches. "The context of teaching and the context of commenting as a private citizen on Twitter are completely different," he insisted. "I would never dream of speaking with students using the same tone and language and rhetoric that I would use on Twitter."

Yet, as Salaita observed, "A speech act is never a neutral thing and how people react to a speech act is not neutral either." This is at the heart of debates over what constitutes a safe space, the current *cri de coeur*, and one of Salaita's on-going concerns.

He believes that any worthy instructor wants to create a rewarding learning environment where all students can speak freely without fear of being ridiculed, devalued or ostracised. And, he noted, the issue isn't restricted to an individual classroom. "The idea of safe space, or student comfort, or trigger warning attaches itself to the idea of student empowerment and I think we need to be attentive to what they want to achieve without being dismissive and find ways to make it jive with our responsibilities as educators."

The problem, as he sees it, arises when an emphasis on safety – or civility – is used by administrators, and sometimes unwittingly by students to limit or invalidate ideas, perspectives, or pedagogy. In Uncivil Rites, Salaita's recent book about the UIUC controversy and its fallout, he writes, "[Civility] is the pretext of the oppressor". Expanding on the idea now, he said: "Civility as maintaining professional decorum is deeply important, but that's not how upper administrators use it. There is something discomfiting about the articulation of politics that are at least tacitly tied into the maintenance of normative viewpoints and hierarchies."

"This", he concluded, "is my beef with the term civility." ⊗

Nan Levinson teaches journalism at Tufts University in Massachusetts and was formerly a US correspondent for Index on Censorship. Her recent book is War Is Not a Game: The New Antiwar Soldiers and the Movement They Built (Rutgers University Press, 2014)

Tools and tricks for truth seekers

45(01): 83/87 | DOI: 10.1177/0306422016643030

Lies and hoaxes spread like wildfire in the age of social media. How can journalists, and readers, avoid being fooled? **Alastair Reid** shares his tips

A GRISLY VIDEO CIRCULATED widely around the internet in 2012. Two men sat bare-chested and terrified against a red brick wall while a figure in military fatigues stood over them, revving a chainsaw. Off camera, someone barked orders in Arabic. The men were brutally murdered.

This video was released by anti-government forces in Syria as evidence of war crimes committed by the Assad regime. But it was not what it seemed. The video originated five years previously in Mexico, where drug cartels have a history of violently executing opponents. It had been cleverly over-dubbed for propaganda purposes, and many fell for its message.

Made-up stories don't just come from lone-wolf hoaxers. Governments from Mexico to Turkey, as well as other political organisations, are becoming adept at using social media for manipulation and misinformation. Journalists have always been expected to use their detective skills to track down sources. But as online reports have the potential to influence the news agenda across the world, far faster than print stories, the potential for falsehoods to circulate as facts is greater than ever. Fortunately, technology has also furnished us with a new set of tools that can help us work out whether those who are telling the story are telling the truth.

Online verification follows the same basic principles established over decades of newsprint: be suspicious of everything, always have more than one source for a claim, and find out the who, what, where, when, why and how. Increasingly, those skills are also being honed by ordinary individuals who want to prod a news story before believing it.

Made-up stories don't just come from lone-wolf hoaxers. Governments are becoming adept at using social media for misinformation

The most common form of digital misinformation is old imagery re-used in the context of a new story. Many major news events are accompanied by recycled pictures. It has happened during the Syrian war with disturbing regularity but was also evident during the Paris attacks in November 2015, the Bamako hostage situation in Mali a week later, and last April's earthquake in Nepal. (Remember the photo of the hugging toddlers that did the rounds after the quake? It was taken in Vietnam in 2007.) →

The quickest way to check the history of a picture on the web is with a reverse image search (that is, a search generated by an image rather than words). Google has archived billions of images, and anyone can upload an image file or paste an image's URL into its search bar to cross-reference the database for any matches. The net can be cast even wider with a Google Chrome plugin called RevEye, which will check databases at Google, TinEye, Bing, Russian web company Yandex and Chinese search engine Baidu. By using these simple tools, many news organisations could have avoided the embarrassment of publishing old pictures as new.

The process is more difficult for video, as cross-referencing every frame in one video with every frame in every video in a database involves supercomputer levels of number crunching. One alternative is to grab the video's thumbnail picture and use it for a reverse image search: this can flag up other videos that contain the same image. Otherwise, searching video networks for keywords associated with your video can bring back results.

Thus, with patience and the right tools, one can generally work out whether a supposedly new image or video has in fact been recycled. More difficult is determining whether images that are new are really showing what they claim to. Of course, tracking down the original uploader and speaking to them directly is the surest way of getting closer to the story; ideally, they will send you the original file.

10 ways journalists can stand up their facts

....

In a world filled with new digital tricks, journalists shouldn't forget traditional verification techniques, says former newspaper editor PETER SANDS

Can you stand it up? Those five words were the ones I probably uttered more than any other when editing a daily newspaper. Excited reporters would be fed a diet of rumours: a member of parliament has left his wife, the chief constable has been suspended. These snippets would then be thrown into the daily news conference. And, with some exaggerated world-weariness, I would ask the key question. Can you stand it up? I never heard about half of the stories again.

Our advantage was that when a lead emerged at midday, we had nine hours to stand it up. If we couldn't make it watertight we could give ourselves another 24 hours. In today's digital world the pressure is on to push the button as soon any unsubstantiated tale flashes across our Twitter feeds. And the rush to publish means half-baked stories, outdated pictures and factual errors appear on websites that should know better. The irony is that verification has never been easier. My staff used to tread a regular path to our library to consult Dod's Parliamentary Companion, Bartholomew's Gazetteer and our own cuttings. Now you can check almost everything online. So why don't we? As Spotlight, the Oscar-winning Hollywood film on investigative journalism shows, sourcing, checking and re-checking is how you nail whether a story stands up. In the world of 24-hour news and digital everything, those traditional techniques should not be forgotten. They include:

1 Be suspicious of everything. Take nothing at face-value. Check for vested interests. Trust no-one – even good contacts.

2 Your job is to confirm things. If you can't, try harder. If you really can't, don't publish.

Failing that, it's worth remembering that every digital camera embeds metadata in the file of a photograph, including the GPS coordinates, the time it was taken and the type of camera used – all vital clues in your investigation. These details can often be viewed by uploading the image to a free site like Jeffrey's Exif Viewer (Exif, which stands for exchangeable image file format, is the technical term for this metadata). Unfortunately no such data is embedded in videos, and social media networks strip out metadata entirely, so that any image which has passed through Facebook, Twitter or the like will have little information to offer. In these cases, more creative techniques are necessary.

Time-consuming as it is, matching locations in footage and reports to satellite imagery often provides the clearest proof of a location. A recent story starkly illustrates this. Russian forces started bombing areas of Syria at the end of September, following a formal request by President Bashar Assad for assistance in fighting rebel and jihadist groups. Soon after, the Russian Ministry of Defence began posting videos of the airstrikes – captured by the bombers as they dropped their payload – to its official YouTube channel.

According to the Russian government, the airstrikes hit IS targets. But following reports from the ground that most of the strikes were targeting non-IS groups, volunteers and journalists at the open-source investigations site Bellingcat decided to investigate. After comparing the ministry's videos with →

---

3 Always go to primary sources. Ask the chief constable if he is being suspended. Ask the authority chairman. If they won't talk, find the committee members – all of them. When my neighbour was killed the local paper splashed it and got three facts wrong. Nobody from the paper had called the family (or me for that matter). Nobody bothered to make the effort. Shocking.

4 Follow the two-sources rule. Get everything verified by at least two trustworthy sources. Ideally on the record.

5 Use experts. There are universities, academics, specialists who will flag up credibility issues. Experts also know other experts.

6 Every story has a paper trail. There are still archives (try LexisNexis), court papers, Company House, Tracesmart. Has the same mistake been made before?

7 Ask yourself the key questions. What else can

I look at? Who else can I talk to? Is it balanced? Did I write the headline first and make the story fit?

8 Make sure the readers understand what is opinion and what is fact. And that includes the headline.

9 Sweat the small stuff. Dates, spelling, names, figures, statistics. Don't forget the who, what, why, where, when and how.

10 Evaluate the risk. There are times when with all the rigorous checking, a story might still only be 99%. If instinct and public interest tell you to publish – pass it to the editor. That is what he or she is paid for. And, with the other nine rules followed thoroughly, hopefully the editor won't need to ask the key question.

Peter Sands is the former editor of UK daily newspaper the Northern Echo and runs media consultancy Sands Media Services

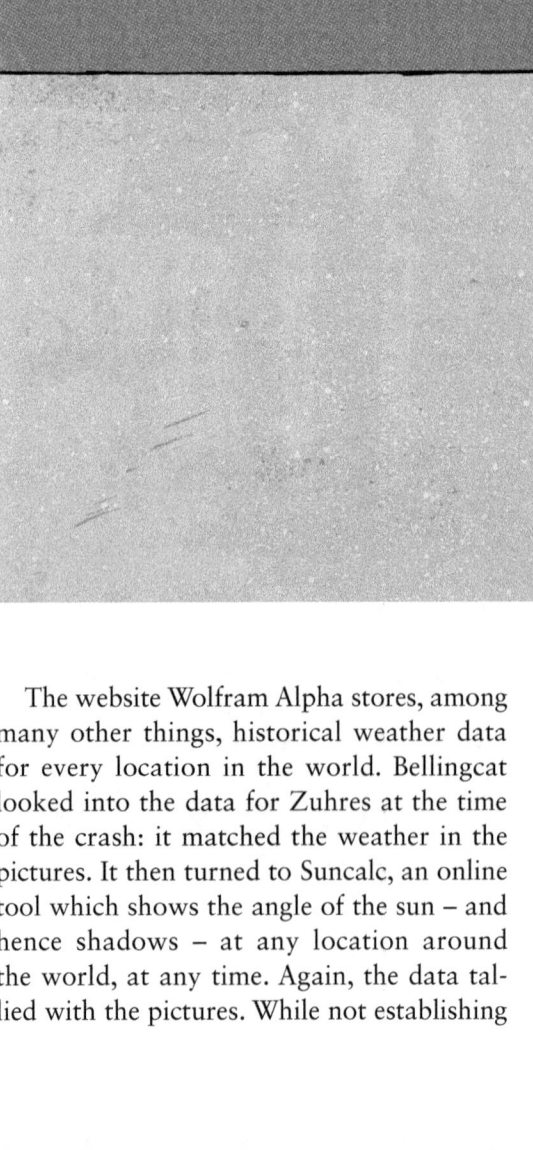

→ satellite imagery of the places they purported to show, they found that only 25% of the strikes verifiably landed where they claimed to – and that the majority of those targets weren't even IS positions to begin with. The rest hit territories held by other groups, in keeping with Assad's request for military support in the country.

However, most pictures from eyewitnesses are taken at street level, so the street-view services on mapping sites like Google and Yandex can play a key role in verifying images. By identifying landmarks and signage in a picture or video, many news organisations have been able to whittle down the list of potential locations until they get a match. Corroborating reports and images are crucial – which is where free tools like Yomapic,

By doing a simple reverse image search on Google, many news organisations could have avoided the embarrassment of publishing old pictures as new

which shows geotagged pictures from social media sites in locations around the world, come in useful.

Establishing that a photo or video was taken at the time claimed by the source is another problem – albeit one that new digital tools can also help establish. The best signifiers of time are those provided by nature: the weather and the angle of the sun. Many have argued that flight MH17 was shot down in July 2014 by a Russian Buk missile. Online sources have provided photos and video of a Buk, and claimed they were taken in the Ukrainian town of Zuhres, some 20 miles from the crash site, on the same day the plane crashed. Maps and landmarks prove the footage was taken in Zuhres, but how can the time be proved?

The website Wolfram Alpha stores, among many other things, historical weather data for every location in the world. Bellingcat looked into the data for Zuhres at the time of the crash: it matched the weather in the pictures. It then turned to Suncalc, an online tool which shows the angle of the sun – and hence shadows – at any location around the world, at any time. Again, the data tallied with the pictures. While not establishing

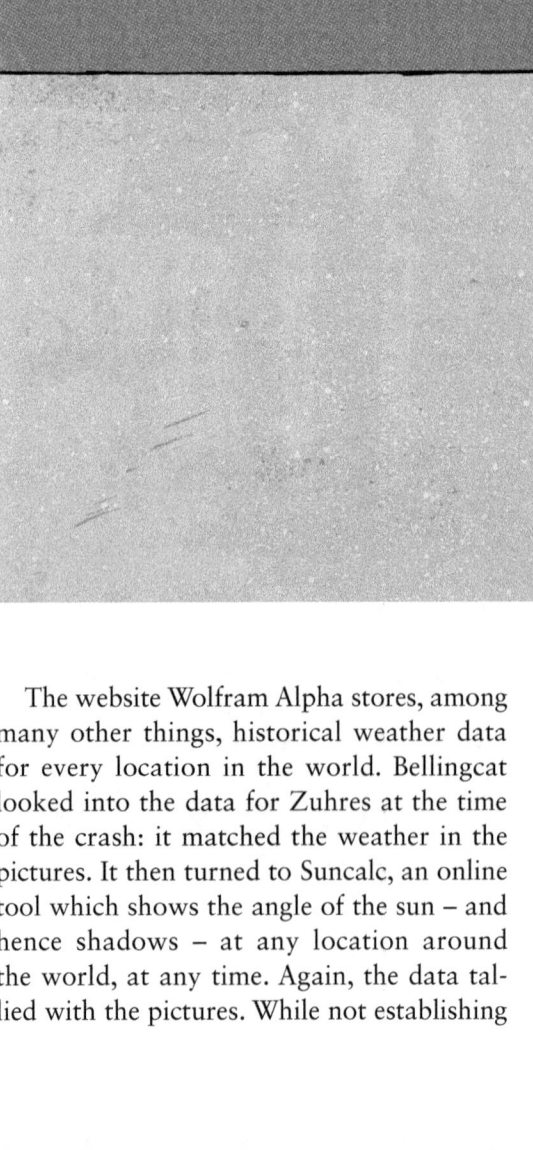
Credit: Eva Bee

cast-iron proof, Bellingcat build a solid case for a Buk launcher being in the right place and time.

The prevalence of smartphones, social media and online connectivity has created powerful new resources for verification of the facts. They also give unprecedented scope for lies and propaganda to spread. As the possibilities for misinformation multiply, it is more important than ever for journalists, and the public generally, to use their analytical and verification skills before they put their trust in the news they are being told. ⊗

Alastair Reid is managing editor of First Draft, a coalition of organisations working with social media and journalism, and specialising in online news gathering and verification. Find out more at firstdraftnews.com

Your television is watching you

45(01): 88/90 | DOI: 10.1177/0306422016643031

From internet-connected TVs to wristbands monitoring our fitness, the things we own are stockpiling information about us. **Jason DaPonte** asks leading privacy adviser **Gilad Rosner** how this affects our freedom to speak and act freely

IN A WORLD where you can exchange texts with your home appliances, where wristbands are monitoring our health and fitness data, and "smart" TVs can record what we say in our own lounges, new possibilities for surveillance and privacy breaches are emerging in ways most consumers can't even imagine. So, how much protection do we have? Gilad Rosner, founder of the Internet of Things Privacy Forum and an adviser to the UK government on privacy, argues that traditional digital privacy practices aren't enough as what he calls the "third wave" of the internet takes hold.

"The first wave of the internet was made up of fixed devices [desktop computers] and the second wave is mobile computing. The internet of things is a third wave that puts connectivity into devices that weren't on networks before," he told Index, citing examples like internet-connected TVs and "smart-home" energy meters.

There are more than 25 billion internet-connected "things" now and this will grow to as many as 50 billion by 2020, according to the US Federal Trade Commission.

So far, most internet privacy policies have been built around consumers agreeing to what data service providers can collect about them but haven't normally touched on just how that data can be used. Rosner and others want to see a shift to a consent-to-use model, similar to those used in the US around personal credit and medical data.

"Internet-of-things devices can amplify the leeching out of data as the devices become more mainstream," said Rosner. The fact that smart meters are able to determine when you're at home or not, to increase your energy efficiency, may not seem sinister, but if this data becomes public and is combined (correctly or incorrectly) with other data, it could be used against you in a criminal hearing to help determine your location during a crime. Location information from a consumer's phone (which consumers are largely happy to share) could also be combined with events data that places them at a protest or event. If this gets into the wrong hands, it could bring them under police surveillance. This could, in turn, lead to false accusations, threats to employment or restrict a person's freedom of expression.

Rosner believes that the power of combining data sets is "too hard to conceptualise [for consumers]. There's no way for people

to envisage their own privacy. The capacity for the devices to contribute to deep and broad profiles of us [the consumer] contributes to the worry about the internet of things because it inputs into the analysis of big data." This is why Rosner is convinced that a consent-to-collect approach to data must shift to a consent-to-use approach, and that simple consumer awareness and education is not enough.

"We're more than the sum of our data, but there are a lot of forces that would drive us towards the commoditisation of ourselves [via our data]," he said. He believes regulation needs to change, but this would be

There are more than 25 billion internet-connected "things" now and this will grow to as many as 50 billion by 2020

complex, provoking accusations from the industry that innovation was being stifled.

The Open Data Institute, a non-profit organisation that connects, enables and inspires people to innovate with all types of data – including open, shared and closed – believes that "both privacy and openness create trust" in relationships between →

WATCH OUT WATCH OUT ... INSPECTOR JACK FROST IS ABOUT! HE'S AFTER YOUR SHOPPING, EATING AND TRAVEL HABITS!

choices in how to use data."

The EU and the USA are taking different approaches towards regulating these new developments. The US approach has been to enact broad-based privacy laws without being technology specific; whereas the EU has come up with more prescriptive laws expected to take effect in 2018. Conflicts between these approaches could still leave consumers feeling confused and disempowered about what happens to their data and how they can control it.

The EU regulation will require companies to use "privacy by design" – a set of principles that takes consumer data protection into account from the start. Rosner, the ODI and Nesta (a UK charity that advocates for innovation and growth) support this as a best practice that can help improve the consumer experience. Using privacy by design could potentially avoid cases like the one where Samsung was accused, in 2015, of having its smart TVs "listening" to customers in their own homes.

The TV manual read: "If your spoken words include personal or other sensitive information, that information will be among the data captured and transmitted to a third party." After a press exposé and a public outcry, the company clarified the legalise. Like other voice-activated services from Apple, Motorola and Amazon, the device didn't start processing data until it "heard" the right command, such as "Hi TV", or had the microphone turned on manually via the remote control.

Rosner remains optimistic that the internet of things can deliver on its promise of empowering consumers without turning into a dystopian nightmare. "Ultimately, I'd like to see the data about us ... treated radioactively," he said. "In that it's understood to be deeply personal and not thrown around and commoditised willy-nilly." ⊗

Jason DaPonte is the founder of consultancy The Swarm and the former head of BBC Mobile

→ customers and companies. "We believe that the value of our data infrastructure can be maximised when we maximise openness but also keep private what should be private," Peter Wells, an associate from the ODI, told Index.

Smart meters are able to determine when you're at home or not ... which could be used against you in a criminal hearing

He added: "The European Union regulations are being strengthened ... but regulation won't deliver informed consent on its own. Internet-of-things services could choose to embrace openness by being prepared for new regulations, being transparent in how they are using data, and by helping both their staff and their customers make better

Tackling Trumbo

45(01): 92/97 | DOI: 10.1177/0306422016643032

Screenwriter **John McNamara** on why he chose to tell the story of
blacklisted Hollywood writer Dalton Trumbo, and how after 25 years in
the movie industry he thought it would be an impossible film to make

PICTURED: Dalton Trumbo, played here by Bryan Cranston, secretly wrote screen hits including Roman Holiday

I DIDN'T WRITE TRUMBO for political reasons, or because I felt I had anything new to say about the dangers of censorship and demagoguery. My interest came about because I was lucky to meet four writers who, for much of their careers, were very unlucky.

The first was Arthur Laurents, best known as the librettist of the musical West Side Story and screenwriter of the first studio movie about the Hollywood Blacklist (albeit a fictional one), The Way We Were. We met in 1982, through the first annual Young Playwrights Festival, a national writing competition founded by composer Stephen Sondheim. Thanks to Steve and his arts foundation, my one-act play and nine others were produced off-Broadway. Arthur was one of the directors. A witty, intimidating, engaging man, I'd nag him for career advice ("Write more than you talk," he'd say) and lessons he learned in his career. On the latter, his replies were less terse.

I loved The Way We Were and it remains one of my favourite movies. Arthur said the experience of making it was painful, not only because he clashed with the director and was fired and rehired more than once, but also because he himself had been blacklisted in the late 1940s and throughout the 1950s for his progressive political beliefs. For him, writing The Way We Were – even in its heavily dramatised form – meant reliving nightmarish agony. He had lost his career because he refused to name fellow radicals; he lost friends because they named him to save their own careers.

I was too young at the time to do much but listen, and that was a good thing, because his anecdotes about loyalty, betrayal, revenge and forgiveness, were the purest educational lectures I'd experienced.

Two years later, while an undergraduate at New York University, I leapt at the chance to audit a graduate screenwriting class taught by Ring Lardner Junior, Waldo Salt and Ian McLellan Hunter, all formerly blacklisted. While I very much wanted to learn what they

Credit: Hilary Bronwyn Gayle

had to teach me about writing, thanks to Arthur I also wanted to learn more about the blacklist from those who'd lived through it.

And so I did, none more so than from Ian McLellan Hunter, who told me that though he was the credited writer of the classic romantic comedy Roman Holiday, he'd been the front for the movie's actual, blacklisted screenwriter: his great friend, Dalton Trumbo.

Trumbo's name then came up frequently in class. He'd only been dead a few years, but his presence still cast a huge shadow. As Ian and Ring described Trumbo's humour in the face of luckless battle – or his largesse while flat broke, or hilarious epistolary clashes with congressmen, producers, stars and banks, the

story was again impressed on me. This all happened. In my country. Not long ago. To these people sitting right in front of me and those they knew. What their stories about Trumbo made even clearer was that, while many had survived the blacklist – which was heroic enough – Dalton Trumbo had actually helped end it. He did it consciously, strategically and with as little fear in his heart as any human being I can imagine.

And yet, when you learn interesting things at a young age, you can easily set them aside. Because life. Because new and shiny. Because girls. Because parties. Because ambition and scrambling to get any job you can as a writer. Which is how I more or less forgot about

When I was ticking off all the reasons no one would ever make his story into a movie, I realised I'd silenced myself as efficiently as any studio or government ever could

Trumbo and the blacklist as soon as I moved to Hollywood in 1984.

Twenty-four years later, deep into a Hollywood writing career of high and lows, I was casually telling my friend, producer Kevin Kelly Brown, about Trumbo's life. Kevin saw it as a possible movie. I only →

ABOVE: The film Trumbo tells of how writer Dalton Trumbo was forced to write films under a false name

→ saw the impossibilities. "The hero is a communist," I said, "It's period, it's political, it's showbiz, there is no sex, no gore, no ticking time bombs or fart-based comic set pieces, no tights, fights or flights and, most damningly, no chance of a lucrative tent pole franchise."

In other words, while my government would have no interest in censoring my attempt to tell this story, I, after a quarter century in the Hollywood marketplace, was censoring myself.

And in that moment, it struck me: my baked-in-Los-Angeles thinking had become not just narrow but cowardly. The best prison a society can construct is made by and for the prisoners. Once I realised this is exactly the kind of future the House Un-American Activities Committee would have dreamed

about, I committed heart and soul to the story of Dalton Trumbo.

Kevin and I optioned Bruce Cook's Dalton Trumbo biography with our own money, and I set about writing and rewriting it on spec for the next seven years.

We soon discovered self-censorship isn't made in a vacuum but born on palm-lined boulevards pulsing with big, sleek cars and people in dark, sleek attire talking to one another on tiny, sleek phones, all on the hunt for The Next Big Thing that, it goes without saying, must be sleek.

Which is the reason the movie output of major studios has primarily narrowed to: big comedies, bigger action movies, biggest family animated films. A movie like Trumbo would not have a place on a major studio's slate, mainly because it doesn't reassure

the audience that its beliefs are sacrosanct; rather it demands they question those beliefs and face the fact that some of life's problems are irresolvable. Superhero problems are resolved by conquering obstacles we all agree on (destruction of Earth – bad; saving babies – good); movie comedians can titillate but mustn't disturb (goofy dad farts uncontrollably at mom's birthday… but shows up for father-daughter dance). There is nothing wrong with the superhero or goofy dad. I take my nine-year-old son to every one of their movies the second they hit the multiplex and enjoy them as much as he does. My only issue is the multiplex really ought to be renamed the uni-plex, because it only shows us the stories we want to believe, rarely the ones we need to confront.

Trumbo had no interest in celebrating the things on which we all agree. In fact, he fought for the opposite, believing each and every American has the right to be wrong.

But this same script that repelled the major studios attracted a sharp and tasteful producer in Michael London, an excellent director in Jay Roach, and stars Bryan Cranston, Helen Mirren, Diane Lane, John Goodman, Michael Stuhlbarg, Louis CK and Elle Fanning, a package of talent that locked down a new financing company, ShivHans, and its distributor, Bleecker Street.

And while rounds of script notes are commonplace at the major studios, as they try to reshape what is true (a communist fights to save the First Amendment) into what might become beloved (a steroidal white male in neoprene kills aliens… farts… and saves babies), ShivHans and Bleecker Street never had a single note on the script.

All the rewriting I did was with the director and actors, under the watchful eyes of our consultants, Trumbo's daughters Niki and Mitzi. Everyone's common goal was to make the movie as honest, accurate and entertaining as possible.

So while Dalton Trumbo the man laboured under such crushing political

oppression he couldn't even put his name on his often-compromised work, Trumbo the movie is exactly as I wrote it, without a breath of compromise, made better at every step by the passionate debates we had along the way. For good or ill, and I'll never be an impartial judge, not a single rewrite on Trumbo dulled its jagged edges or resolved

The multiplex should be renamed the uni-plex, because it only shows the stories we want to believe, rarely the ones we need to confront

its inherent contradictions.

It may be the pinnacle of irony that a movie about fascistic politicians and paranoid movie studios of 1947 colluding to kill progressive thought would be made in 2015 under circumstances of unregenerate artistic freedom.

It's an irony I think Dalton Trumbo would smile at knowingly. His genius and bullheaded love of fighting and winning led to the removal of a muzzle that silenced an entire nation.

In part because of Dalton Trumbo, I live in a country that's arguably more free (though with far more surveillance). Yet in that moment when I was ticking off all the reasons no one would ever make his story into a movie, I realised I'd silenced myself as efficiently as any studio or government ever could. I'm glad his life and work helped me see that. And that by writing his story, I could remove the muzzle I'd placed on myself. In late-night quiet, I promise him – a prayer from one atheist to another – that I'll never willingly slip that muzzle on myself again. And will fight anyone who tries to force it on another. ⊗

John McNamara is the screenwriter of the new film Trumbo, *currently in cinemas*

CULTURE

In this section

PICTURED: Basque musician Fermin Muguruza performs at Coogee Diggers in Sydney,
Australia, August 2013

Know your enemy

45(01): 100/108 | DOI: 10.1177/0306422016643033

Akram Aylisli was celebrated as the People's Writer of Azerbaijan, until he upset the government. Yet despite having his books burnt and a reward issued to anyone who would cut off his ear, he continues to write. **John Angliss** introduces an abridged version of Aylisli's latest short story, The Polecat, published here in English for the first time

THIS WINTER, RENEWED skirmishes on the border between Armenia and Azerbaijan led to fears that the long-standing tension between them was esclating again. At the centre of the conflict is not only historically significant territory (Nagorno-Karabagh), but also two competing narratives, with nationalists on both sides telling stories of horrific pogroms against their communities when the Soviet Union began to crumble.

Akram Aylisli, a writer well-known for his plays and novels set in the villages of Azerbaijan, decided instead to tell a different story. In his 2012 novella Stone Dreams, he fictionalised the massacres of Armenians from 1918 to 1989 through the perspective of the Azeris involved, both the perpetrators and those trying to save their Armenian neighbours.

The reaction to Aylisli's taboo-breaking story was sharp. His plays were banned from theatres; his books were burnt; his literary awards were revoked; and the head of the governing party offered a reward to anyone who would cut off Aylisli's ear.

"The government tried every possible way to destroy me, but I endured every type of persecution and I did not leave my homeland," he told Index on Censorship from his home in Baku.

Years after allowing Stone Dreams to be published in a Russian literary magazine, he is still facing persecution. "The dreadful sanctions employed against me and my family remain in force. Officials whom I have known for years are still frightened to say hello to me," he said. "I am automatically banished from everything under the control of the state. My children lost their jobs. Despite this I am still resisting, because I have thousands of readers in this country and, most of all, we owe them gratitude for bringing me where I am."

Asked whether he believes that village literature – a genre that has defined his career – will die out as people continue to migrate to cities, Aylisli said it may have a positive effect "for village literature too is formed in the cities".

Aylisli's latest short story, The Polecat, is the story of Qubuş, a very ordinary man in a fast-depopulating post-Soviet village. It touches upon the brutality of the crowd and the causes of apparently senseless violence, but also includes elements of slapstick humour, a fascination with nature, and forbidden love.

"I don't find Qubuş a romantic. He is a simple, conscientious and moral man who is spiritually tied to village life," said Aylisli. →

"I also share many of the same qualities."

The story takes its name from an incident where Qubuş witnesses villagers killing a polecat and is left traumatised by their brutality.

Aylisli explained: "In Azerbaijan, a polecat is a rare and mystical animal. What people know of them is mostly hearsay. This metaphor contains a hidden philosophical message. People maul a living creature, without knowing what it is and why exactly they need to destroy it."

The Polecat

By Akram Aylisli

1

QUBUŞ WAS DAZZLED by the starlight in the sky in his dream. When he was a small boy, Qubuş had liked nothing more in the boiling summer heat than to stretch out on their sod roof and gaze at the stars in the sky, but back then he had never seen this many stars or this much light.

Then, somehow, the stars suddenly went out. All the light vanished from the world. The sky went instantly darker than dark, like the burnt underside of the metal disk on which his wife Batula baked bread every day. The thought crossed Qubuş's mind that the stark darkness would remain forever, and so in terror, he shook off his sleep and opened his eyes.

The moon had set, but after the complete darkness of the sky in Qubuş's dream, the room seemed even more radiant than most nights. By now, the house was cold. In her own bed, Batula was snuggled up tightly in a blanket.

For a long time Qubuş had woken up in the middle of the night whether he had had a nightmare or not. He would get up and wander around outside, then return to his bed to sleep once more.

In the light of day, those nights under the starry rural skies appeared extraordinary to Qubuş, like a separate world having nothing to do with the village, incredibly far away and high above. The village belonged to everyone by day, but by night was only Qubuş's.

This year, some of those who in other years would have sealed their windows and doors as the cold descended and gone to spend winter in the city, were still in the village. Such a mild autumn had not been seen for a long time. Even if the nights were a little cold, the sun's heat was sufficient for everyone to go out to other houses or the fields. A number of the houses,

ABOVE: Writer Akram Aylisli upset the Azerbaijani government with his 2012 novella Stone Dreams, in which he fictionalised the massacres of Armenians from 1918 to 1989 through the perspective of the Azeris involved

which would soon go dark when seasonal city-dwellers left, still burned their night lamps on their porches until the break of day.

Qubuş's eyes wandered out to the courtyard and fixed on Sona's house for a long time, dreamily watching the weak flame of the lone lamp burning on her porch.

Sona was not from the village; she was a newcomer. She came to marry a man at least 30 years older than her. After she got used to the villagers, she began to tell everyone: "I was married twice in my own village, but my husbands threw me out because I did not have children."

"After two husbands, who in my own village would take me?" she said. "Rather than grow old alone, I said, give me a husband – I don't care if he's aged or crippled."

Qubuş had first seen Sona at least 20 years before on that porch. His heart had leapt when he saw her. How strange the magical, sweet passion that was aroused in him; a new world cast light into his heart.

Back then Qubuş was a little older than 50; now he was past 70. In that time, so many things had happened in the world. The *kolkhoz* [collective farm] had dissolved. Sona's husband Müslüm, the one-time horse manager on the *kolkhoz*, became unemployed and got a chest disease from smoking three to four packs a day.

After Müslüm's first wife died, his daughter, who had married a man in a far-off village, brought Sona, who was the same age as her, to her father. Within a year, God favoured Sona with a perfectly healthy child from the aged, asthmatic Müslüm.

Then suddenly, neither the child remained, nor Sona's former happiness and beauty. But nonetheless, the magical, sweet passion that had made Qubuş's heart leap when he first saw her lived on.

Qubuş had once (while Müslüm was still healthy) almost given in to his passion.

That day, Müslüm was not in the village. Sona was left at home alone.

Qubuş gingerly looked into her courtyard. He saw her lying on the dry earth in the shadow of the apricot tree in front of the porch. She got up, leaned against the tree and looked at Qubuş rapt. Then smiled. It was such a smile that Qubuş's heart filled to the brim with joy, his soul gained untold strength, and an extraordinary light flooded his eyes. He then understood that Sona too had nourished a secret hope. But it turned out that Qubuş would not fulfil the desire that had long lurked in his heart. As he left the house that day, Qubuş's mother, Xavar, had somehow known where he was going.

Suddenly, there was an earsplitting clanging and clattering of an iron spade from behind Sona's fence: Xavar had ostensibly brought it out to clean the gravel and stones from a nearby ditch. She went behind the door of Sona's courtyard and let out such an ugly "ahhem-ahhem" that it put the Müslüm's three-to-four-packs-of-Pamir-a-day "ahem-ahem" to shame. Realising what was going on, Sona plunged into the house.

Qubuş stood a moment unmoving in the shade of the apricot tree before returning →

home in distress.

"You scoundrel! You scoundrel!"

As soon as Qubuş got in the gate, his mother began cursing him from afar. From that day on, Qubuş would often hear the same thing from the old woman. But she never spoke of it to anyone else. As strange as it may sound, it never occurred to Batula that Qubuş might have harboured such desires.

2

AND THEN THE hard days began for Sona. Her son Aslan, who went on military service in April, was sent back in a coffin at the end of May. The fire in her eyes, fuelled by her heart's vigour, went out forever. She mourned and cried, pouring her heart out to everyone she met, blaming her husband Müslüm for the death of her son.

"You know, I told him. I told him a thousand times that that boy would not make a soldier. Take whatever is in the house and sell it, but keep him out of the military – I mean, take the lot and use the money to get him a doctor's note. He wasn't sick, I mean, but my son wasn't one of those boys who could go and serve like a proper soldier. The senile old man didn't listen to me."

There were many in the village who had predicted that Aslan would not carry out his military service to the end and return safely. Others thought he might get a sharp shock and come back a "real man". You see, Aslan wasn't just any child: he was a great source of trouble for the whole village. There wasn't a child that Aslan hadn't harassed and made cry, no old man or woman he hadn't terrorised. The little tyrant would run men over on his horse. He would gallop up and down, grabbing young women's scarves from their heads and waving them in the air like flags.

For maybe more than a year, Sona went to the cemetary every day, in the cold of winter and heat of summer, and sat crying at her son's grave from morning to night.

Recently, Batula had heard from someone that Sona would not stay in the village that winter; she intended to go to stay with her sister who had married in Baku. For now, Sona's lamp was still a lovely sight on the porch, showing she was still there.

3

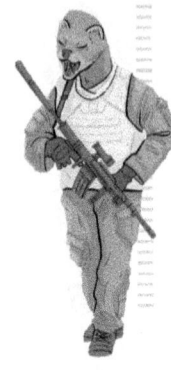

OVER THE PAST 20 or 30 years, one by one the young people of the village had gone off and left. They had found jobs in the shops and bazaars of Baku, Moscow and other Russian cities, then gradually enticed their kith and kin to stay with them. Qubuş feared the time would come when no living soul would be left. In the last two years, this fear had grabbed him tighter. Maybe this was why he had recently been having nightmares every night.

Tonight, when Qubuş returned from the courtyard to lie down in bed, he saw such a terrifying dream that even the world's most horrible tales could not match it.

An empty village; a day without sun. And at the crack of dawn, an uncountable chine of polecats, queued up one behind the other, were making their way slowly into the village from the outskirts. Their target and their intentions were clear: four or five months before, polecats had been mercilessly tortured and killed in the centre of the village – an event which still haunted Qubuş's dreams – and these polecats had come to take revenge on humans.

The hideous, vengeful polecat army had not yet reached the centre of the village when Qubuş saw another battalion of the animals emerge as if from nowhere and barge into the courtyard, killing all the sheep, ripping them apart and gnawing on their flesh. One of the polecats leant against the gateway, staring with blood-red eyes at Batula, who was sweeping in front of the porch. It was awaiting its chance to charge.

Batula, however, suspected nothing.

Qubuş couldn't find the voice to shout or the strength to move in order to save his wife from the polecat's claws. And this time when he awoke to find everything in its proper place, Qubuş went out into the courtyard feeling relieved.

Batula was baking bread on a metal disk below the balcony. The sun was in its place. The sky was in its place.

Qubuş approached his wife and, when he saw the metal plate on the stove, he remembered the deep dark sky from his dream. "Who will I go and see in the village centre?" Qubuş asked, looking up at the transparent, strikingly lit sky. "Will I see Yunus the lawyer? I thought he was an honorable man, but after that polecat incident he lost all my respect. He didn't carry it out humanely, he was ruthless. What do those animals do to anyone that deserves such brutal treatment?"

Qubuş would not forget the torn hide, broken ribs and bloody flesh if he lived another 100 years. The incident happened in the middle of summer, and afterwards Qubuş was so disgusted by that place that he did not set foot there again.

"Yunus is not a bad man. Don't use Yunus as an excuse. You were so afraid that day you haven't shown your face since," Batula said, laughing. "They say you were like that as a child, an awful coward."

"Why don't you slaughter that sheep?" Batula said, after putting a plate of fried eggs in front of her husband. "My mother-in-law, poor woman, died wanting for meat."

"Who should I get to butcher it? There's no butcher left in the village."

"You haven't even thought of going to visit the poor woman's grave for a long time. I go every Thursday," Batula sighed, then stared for a while at the gate.

All the people who would gather in the centre of the village were Qubuş's age. At some time in the past they had been children playing knucklebones together. Now those people came to boast and brag in front of each other. They wore suits and had mobile phones in their pockets. When their telephones rang, they would quickly run to one side and whisper into them, then return to brag some more. "That call came from Moscow," they would →

say. They didn't care what their children were doing in those Moscow shops and bazaars to make money or what trickery they were resorting to. Everyone, old and young, had forgotten how to till their own soil and earn an honest crust.

Qubuş was originally a carpenter: he worked his father's trade. Most of the windows and doors in the village were his handiwork. Now no-one built their homes in the village, there was no work for Qubuş, but he was never without employment. He always found work for himself in the garden or around the house. When he had nothing to do, he would make a rolling-pin, a bread board or some other useful thing for his poor neighbours.

4

THAT AFTERNOON, ON his way to the graveyard, Qubuş was forced to pass by the centre of the village, for there was no other road leading there. Qubuş hoped to come across Sona. He didn't meet anyone, but he both talked to himself and to an imaginary Sona. All the way to the cemetary, they exchanged sweet words.

As he stood with headstones all around, one of the fresh ones stood out. Aslan's picture looked out with such crazy passion you half-expected him to force his way off the stone, jump on a horse and run someone down.

"You scoundrel! You scoundrel!"

This time it was his mother's voice that seemed to come from this world.

By the time Qubuş turned back from the cemetary sunset was nearing. Soon the village centre would fill with bragging men. For now, Yunus the lawyer was sitting alone in the square, listlessly fingering his prayer beads.

Yunus was one of the best-looking men in the village. For 40 years he had chauffeured for the First Secretary of the local district committee. When the government fell and the district committee was abolished, he moved quickly to privatise the brand-new Qaz-24 he had been driving by putting it into his own name. Now Yunus drove every day to the district centre to sit and pass the time with his old friends and acquaintances. From time to time he would help not only those going to the station or to weddings and funerals, but also those needing to go urgently to hospital, whether they could pay or not. For many years, Yunus had taught the people of the village to write petitions and where to take their complaints: this is why they called him Yunus the lawyer.

Qubuş wanted just to greet Yunus and leave, but Yunus was not going to let him.

"Hey, Qubuş, where have you been? Sit down. Tell us you're not tied to your wife's apron strings, you never leave the house."

"I have a lot to do at home," he said. He could find nothing else to say, but he was glad to have the opportunity to ask Yunus about the polecat. "I've been wanting to ask you something for a long time. Where did you catch that polecat you brought here once?"

Yunus studied Qubuş's face suspiciously.

"I ran it over, then I tied it to the car. Both its back legs were broken. But the pest still tried to run off. When I saw it would escape, I tied it up by its head, fastened it to the back of the car, then quickly drove here and took it out so those who had never seen one could see its nasty face. But the burning had nothing to do with me — as you clearly saw yourself. When Manaf the teacher saw that Abdulla the Black-Arse was here too, he ran to his house to get petrol and poured it on the polecat. Then he set it on fire."

Yunus burst out into loud peals of laughter. "He knew that this would burn Abdulla the Black-Arse as well. I saw myself how hatefully Manaf glowered at Abdulla as that creature burned away."

Abdulla the Black-Arse was one of the richest men in the village and he had married Samaya, the village's most beautiful girl. Manaf the teacher was madly in love with her, and the marriage drove a hot brand into the poor man's heart. The people of this village were so difficult that everyone harboured malice towards someone.

"A polecat is a real pest," said Yunus. "There's no nastier animal on the face of the earth. They are such dishonourable animals that they will dig up corpses and eat them."

"Have you seen polecats dig up corpses yourself?"

"No, I haven't. I heard it from my father."

"Obviously your father must have heard it from his father. This is just a story, it's nonsense. People have been living in this village for thousands of years, and no one has yet seen a polecat desecrate a corpse. It's an old habit of idle people the world over to put the truth aside and talk of fictions."

Neither could find anything to say for a while.

"I'm raising a beautiful yearling sheep for roasting. Can you come and butcher it in the morning," Qubuş had no idea how such a thing had suddenly occurred to him.

Yunus looked completely astonished: "Qubuş, are you seeing straight? When did I become a butcher? I've never in my life so much as slaughtered a chicken. If you like, I'll find a man from the town tomorrow to come and slaughter your sheep. If you give him a kilo of meat, he'll be happy."

"I will, in fact I'll give him three kilos. You find someone and bring him in the morning, and you'll get a nice share of meat too."

"You can be sure of it," said Yunus, determined.

They ran out of words.

Qubuş decided it was time to go. It wasn't long until the morons with their mobile phones came out of their houses to swagger over. But instead of getting up to go home, Qubuş had a vision of Aslan's sly eyes, with their crazy passion, among the fresh gravestones.

"Maybe you will know, Yunus," he said. "Where did Sona have Aslan's gravestone made?"

"Sona didn't have Aslan's gravestone made, I did," Yunus said with unconcealed pride. "I saw her off. She packed up and left for Baku this past Sunday."

Qubuş felt a dark wind rushing through his heart.

"Impossible! But her lamp was burning all night."

"She left it like that on purpose. If my son should suddenly arrive, she said, let him not see the house unlit. She still wants to believe he is away on military service."

Qubuş said nothing to his wife about Sona when he came home.

"I saw Yunus the lawyer in the centre of the village," he said. "He promised to find us someone from the town to kill the sheep in the morning. That lawyer is a real lawyer. Look what he told me: he said that everyone who goes out to the village centre has a big devil inside of them. They all hate one another. The man who set fire to that polecat, in his own mind, was burning his enemy. It's difficult for a person to believe these things, but some lap it up."

Batula found what Qubuş said quite funny. Laughing, she said: "You were there that day too. Maybe one or two of those people were burning with rage for you."

Qubuş didn't take his wife's laughter seriously, continuing with his previous earnestness: "Why one or two?" he said. "Almost all of them!"

"Bah! Why would that many hate you? Who've you done any wrong to?"

"Enmity doesn't only happen when people do wrong."

"Then where does it come from?"

Qubuş had long known the answer to this question, but he was in no hurry to tell Batula. He looked silently at his wife for a time. "It comes from me not being like any of them," he said, his heart knowing that if a polecat resembled other animals, maybe the villagers would not have persecuted it so much.

5

THAT NIGHT, QUBUŞ did not go out into the courtyard. He did not want to see the single lamp burning on Sona's porch, because for Qubuş, the burning light now meant that Sona would never return to the village. What was the relationship between Sona putting that light on the porch when returning to Baku and whether or not she would return? Qubuş didn't know. But despite not having gone to school, he knew that in this world, there are some things the eye cannot see; only the heart can.

August 2015 ⊗

Akram Aylisli is a playwright and novelist
Translated by John Angliss and Denis Ferhatović

Culture | Courses | Collections

Bishopsgate Institute is home to a programme of courses and cultural events. We also hold archive collections on London, radicalism, protest and LGBT history, including the Index on Censorship archive.

Conveniently located, and housed in a Grade II* listed building, we provide a welcoming space for independent thinkers. Our library is free to use and open to all.

Bishopsgate Institute | 230 Bishopsgate | London | EC2M 4QH
@bishopsgateinst /Bishopsgate Institute bishopsgate.org.uk

Borderless bard

45(01): 110/111 | DOI: 10.1177/0306422016643034

Poet **Edin Suljic** talks to **Josie Timms** about why he recast Shakespeare as a bingo addict and brandy lover who is struggling in a war zone

POET EDIN SULJIC has spent the last 24 years living in London. He left the former Yugoslavia in 1991, fleeing the country ahead of the impending war. His poem My Mate Shakespeare is being published for the first time in Index on Censorship magazine.

Having visited his homeland last summer, Edin saw a relentless stream of desperate refugees, and this inspired the poem. "I am begging him, my Mate Shakespeare, to come back to his strength, particularly now when everybody wants to celebrate his life. One portion of the wretched humanity is directly responsible for the misery of the others and he, Shakespeare, needs to be here to show the

wretched through the laughter and tears that the suffering of others actually hurts," he said.

Suljic is involved with theatre group Bards Without Borders, which uses Shakespeare as an inspiration for productions themed around migration. "When I was young I was in a youth group for the national theatre in my home town. We did two productions of Shakespeare plays, A Midsummer Night's Dream and Comedy of Errors, just like we are doing at Bards Without Borders."

Shakespeare was known for ridiculing politicians and Suljic believes that theatre is an ideal way to take on such issues, and use comedy. "I think we need more plays which

ABOVE: Poet Edin Suljic has spent 24 years in London since leaving former Yugoslavia. His poem My Mate Shakespeare reflects his experience of war and life as a refugee

attack these issues," he said. "The way to do it is to ridicule, to expose it. Through sincere work we constantly have to push these boundaries that the majority imposes on us."

Suljic said: "In My Mate Shakespeare he's a broken man because I don't think we can go much longer with these wars. Even Shakespeare today would be in a state of desperation when he thinks about the world we live in now."

My Mate Shakespeare

The first time I met Shakespeare, he looked nothing like himself, nothing like that
    depiction of a poster boy with a hipster beard one comes across every so often.
No, he was tall, scrawny, flamboyant, thin-moustached and bespectacled, with large
    hands into which his guitar almost disappeared as he sang perched on a low
    stool, in the theatre's green room, where we would occasionally be allowed to
    sneak into as aspiring writers and actors, to join the post-press-night party.
In those days we shared many breakfasts, mainly a coffee and cigarettes, and
    sometimes a boiled egg given to us by a kind cook in the theatre's canteen.
And our fortunes took many turns …
Some claimed his work as if it was their own, they complained about too many foreigners
    in his plays (As if we don't have our own trulls – they'd say). Others even claimed he
    never wrote anything, or worse, that he never existed. My mate Shakespeare …
Every so often he'd ask me if I am still writing, then say:
    – Keep writing, keep writing, me duck …
But then, he ripped apart my first play.
That's too serious boyo – he said, and inserted an innuendo into every second paragraph.
He was madly in love with this blonde, petite, round-eyed actress who was patiently
    waiting for her lucky break on stage, and for him to come to her garret.
Almost addicted to bingo and drinking a lot of poor-quality brandy, he got himself into
    many troubles by attacking so many kings, offending so many celebrities and ridiculing
    politicians; and he wrote too many plays about deformity and cross dressing.
Even his small girlfriend turned out to be a man in disguise.
Then the war tore everything apart, and I haven't seen him since.
    The world entered into this never-ending war.
I heard the stories … He married a very different girl and they had two beautiful
    children and they lived somewhere in the outskirts of the City.
He doesn't go to the theatre anymore.
But then, like most stories about him, these too, turned out to be unreliable.
    I saw him once more – in the East End. That last time I saw him, he
    looked like a broken man. My friend. My indestructible friend.
Something or somebody managed to do it to him.
I suppressed a cry inside myself. What is left for the rest of us? What
    will happen to us if people like him could be broken?
Then he leaned over his glass of cheap brandy and whispered
    – Keep writing, keep writing, boyo … ⊗

Josie Timms is Index on Censorship's editorial assistant

Singing for Tahrir

45(01): 112/115 | DOI: 10.1177/0306422016643036

Egypt's security officers arrested **Ramy Essam** for singing at protests in Tahrir Square. He was imprisoned and tortured. Here we publish the lyrics to one of his songs in English for the first time, and **Vicky Baker** talks to him about returning home

"**I HAVE MADE MY** final decision. Whether it is risky or not, I need to go back and continue what I started," Egyptian musician Ramy Essam told Index on Censorship on the phone from Sweden where he currently lives in exile.

Essam rose to fame suddenly during Egypt's 2011 revolution when he took his guitar to a stage in Cairo's Tahrir Square and turned protest chants into rock songs, provoking mass sing-a-longs and some of the most enduring images of the uprising.

Soon his story – which included being tortured by soldiers in the Egyptian Museum after Tahrir Square was cleared – was known worldwide. The New Yorker called him "the bard of the Egyptian Revolution" and he featured prominently in the 2013 Oscar-nominated documentary The Square. But fame also brought new enemies and he started to become concerned about impending military service, which is compulsory for Egyptian men under 30. "People [in the military] were sending me threats on social media and on

OPPOSITE: Musician Ramy Essam went into exile after being arrested and tortured by the Egyptian army during the 2011 uprising in Tahrir Square

Credit: Ahmed Roshdy

Credit: David Brook / Festival 800

I wasn't politically active. I was just a guy who didn't like what was going on, someone who believes in the power of music to change

my phone, saying 'We're waiting for you'. This is their best chance to catch me. If I am serving as a soldier, they can use military laws on me."

A two-year Safe Havens arts scholarship, awarded by the Swedish city of Malmö in 2014, came at the right time. Now aged 28, he plans to stay in Europe until he turns 30 in June 2017, and then can return home. "If they won't let me play and I have to take my guitar to go underground, I'll do that," he said. "The first time we called for change

instantly, we were very dreamy, but we can be more realistic now. It may take 10 or 20 years, but at least we have started."

Living abroad means he is less famous now in his homeland, but he keeps in touch with his core fan base online. "I am not there physically, but my music and my voice is still with there with them," he insisted. This year he plans to release a new album, which will bring together some of his acoustic songs but with higher production values, thanks to support he is receiving in Sweden.

One of the tracks on the album is called A Letter to the Security Council in the UN, which is a collaboration with Egyptian poet Amgad El Qahwagy, who he often works with. (Essam typically writes the melodies, while Qahwagy writes the lyrics.) The lyrics, which are published here in English for the

A letter to the Security Council in the UN

Lyrics by Amgad El Qahwagy

I am pleading that my words reach you.
Despite your concern
To the Security Council of the United Nations
This is not my first message
This is me the bloody human
Rulers sharpening their swords using ignorance over my silence
Out of darkness injustice was created
I became one without any knowledge, following my obsessions
I befriended my enemy
Not even knowing my own flaws
I became stranger in my own journey
Others reading my compasses for me
Ignorance navigating me
Oh, my lord, secretary of the council, and all secretaries betraying my dreams
I might not understand the words on my TV
But I know that prison's air is heavy
I might not know how to spell freedom
But I carry its meaning with me
I know that today will pass by
But tomorrow I might break free
Oh my lord, watch out for me!

first time, were inspired by the United Nation's annual day of literacy. "After the revolution we started to lose the battle because of illiterate and uneducated people. Dictators use this to control people," Essam explained. "This song is about a poor person who is confused about who is an enemy and who is a friend, but just wants to be free. The message is: I don't know how to write about freedom but I still have it in me."

Essam's most famous song Irhal, meaning "leave", was his 2011 call for then president Hosni Mubarak to resign. He blended chants heard in the square with his own refrains. "I wasn't politically active at the time," he confessed. "I was just a guy who didn't like what was going on, and someone who believes in the power of music to change."

The musician said he has been criticised for being too optimistic, but he said he is inspired by his fans, who are mostly teenagers. "This new generation aren't listening to TV or radio, or reading newspapers," he said. "The ways they controlled my generation no longer work. We have a new kind of freedom. We have the chance to make a difference. This is what gives me hope."

Vicky Baker is deputy editor of Index on Censorship magazine

Notes of discord

45(01): 116/118 | DOI: 10.1177/0306422016643037

Basque musician **Fermin Muguruza** is currently banned from holding concerts in Madrid. He speaks to **Rachael Jolley** about Spain, his music and the political reactions to it

own record label Esan Ozenki and film company Talka Records and Films.

He began playing music at an early age. "The accordion was my first instrument when I was eight years old. Then, any song with lyrics could have a double meaning, like Christmas songs about children coming back home to speak about freedom for political prisoners. Little by little I started listening to protest songwriters clandestinely."

Today he chronicles his reality with singing: "In the years of political transition from dictatorship, the songs of my bands were one of the few ways to tell the unofficial versions of what happened. A lieutenant colonel of the Guardia Civil accused me in a judicial proceeding of 'staining his honour'. There followed 10 years of trials – I won when he was sent to prison in 2000."

But censorship has not disappeared from his life. During the presidency of José María Aznar, long after Franco's demise in 1975, Muguruza was banned from playing in certain cities around Spain.

"When Aznar was president, in 2003, I was touring. The tour became critical of the closure of the only newspaper in the Basque language, the ecological disaster of the tanker Prestige, and the pretence of going to war against Iraq, with Blair and Bush. Aznar banned me, saying I was supporting terrorists.

"After this, I was not allowed to play in a lot of cities of Spain [those cities governed by Aznar's Partido Popular], even if I have a lot of fans who want to come and enjoy my concerts," he said.

He is hopeful that ban may soon be lifted, but in the meantime he can tour around the world and sing in probably the oldest language in Europe, Basque. "Songs are our legacy, our historical memory. We can lose wars, but generations that do not know us will be able to sing our songs." ⊗

Rachael Jolley is the editor of Index on Censorship magazine. She tweets @londoninsider

LEFT: Fermin Muguruza performs at a concert held in Kreuzberg, Berlin, in May 2013

FERMIN MUGURUZA WAS born in 1963 under the fascist regime of Franco. At that time Basque culture was banned – even the language itself was illegal. "Any kind of artistic protester was pursued and condemned with torture and jail," he told Index.

But the period also inspired his music: "After the death of Franco, the punk-rock movement exploded in my mind and I formed my first band called Kortatu, first singing in Spanish and then, when I learned my own language, in Basque."

Muguruza went on to form the band Negu Gorriak in the 1990s, followed by his

Hitz egin

Talk!

Yeah, I also have done
Recitals of bertolt brecht.
I was speaking out
Loud against injustice.
For sure my talk
Bothered them
And they decided
To cut my tongue out.

My hands started
To write freely,
Playing the guitar,
My rebel friend
And again
They came after me, and
They left me armless,
Handicapped.

All in vain,
I soon got to figure
How to do things
With my toes.
But my gaze
Must have seemed
To be damning to them
Because the crows
Plucked out my eyes

My mere presence
Must have unnerved them.
My ears only heard
The gunshot.
Will someone raise
Their voice?
By then, however,
Everyone was mute.

Talk!
For freedom of expression!
Talk!

Shoot the Singer

Shoot the singer

From the snake pit, the two-
headed snakes bite, insult,
Spit and spill their venom

It's funny how comments flare
Easy target, the gunfight's contagious
Shoot at the pianist too,
As a tribute to Truffaut,
And at everyone that moves
within the picture
Who is a threat to them
"Every time you hear the word
culture, pull out your gun"
Learn the lessons from Goebbels' manual

Shoot the singer
From the snake pit, the two-
headed snakes bite, insult,
Spit and spill their venom

Fermin Muguruza has just released a new album recorded in New Orleans, along with a documentary featuring musicians discussing the city 10 years after Hurricane Katrina

X

Index around the world

INDEX NEWS

45(01): 119/121 | DOI: 10.1177/0306422016643038

From a new multimedia project for young people to debate freedom and liberty, to a fundraiser for persecuted musicians, **Josie Timms** looks at the highlights of Index's work over the past three months

TWENTY-ONE YOUNG PEOPLE aged between 16 and 21 gathered at the Index on Censorship offices to kick off the What a Liberty! project in February. The project is inspired by the Magna Carta, one of the most famous documents in the world.

Helen Galliano, producer of What a Liberty!, said: "This five-month project is a fun and innovative way for young people to interact with this ancient document and find out its relevance today. We will be giving the group a platform to discuss freedom and liberty and their ideas of what that means." Seventeen participants have been shortlisted to receive digital, film and editing training to help them create their own Magna Carta 2.0, a multimedia work inspired by their debates. The 17 also travelled to see one of the oldest copies of the Magna Carta at Lincoln Cathedral, as part of this Heritage Lottery-funded project. Later in the year, they will visit schools and youth groups around London to talk at about their findings.

After the first session, one of the participants, Alisia Usher, 16, said: "It was nice to articulate my ideas about these issues and hear other conflicting ideas, and to compare them to others from my age group. It's good to be working on a new Magna Carta as you get to see what is important in society."

Earlier in the year, Index on Censorship magazine celebrated the launch of its What's the Taboo? special issue, with a debate at the Royal Vauxhall Tavern, London. Special guests included comedians Shazia Mirza and Grainne Maguire, film historian Kunle Olulode, and consultant Max Wind-Cowie, who went head to head on tricky subjects, including suicide and grief, mental health, sex and racism.

After joking how a mental illness is almost a requirement to be a stand-up comedian, Maguire told the audience: "In certain careers you're supposed to be macho and mental illness is still seen as a sign of weakness. I just think that's really depressing and sad. →

BELOW: Participants in Index's What a Liberty! workshop, Sarah Michaels, Che Applewhaite and Darshan Leslie, presenting their ideas

→ I think you should be allowed to be vulnerable, but I don't think we are there yet."

Dealing with offence on social networks was the main talking point at the latest meeting of Index's youth advisory board, with concerns raised about who bans accounts and how regulation could be misused.

The group hold monthly online discussions to debate current freedom of expression issues from a global perspective. The eight members, from countries all over the world, including Brazil, Germany and Kenya, will hold their seats on the board

Special guests included comedians Shazia Mirza and Grainne Maguire, film historian Kunle Olulode, and writer Max Wind-Cowie

until June 2016. Applicants for the next six-month intake are encouraged to apply via Index's website, which also has full biographies of the current board. Members include Mariana Cunha e Melo, an associate lawyer in Rio de Janeiro; Emily Carlotta Wright, an independent filmmaker and journalist working on a film in Bogotá about Colombia's disappeared; and Ephraim Kenyanito, who is a policy fellow at AccessNow.org in Kenya.

Index's Mapping Media Freedom project, which tracks media violations across EU member states and neighbouring countries, was upgraded in January and now has an alert feature, so users can receive updates themed by country or type of attack. For example, you could receive an email each time a threat is reported against a female journalist in Germany, if you choose those as your alert terms.

MMF's quarterly report, released in February, showed that 518 people had lost their jobs at both public and private media outlets across Europe from October to December 2015. Around 188 of these positions were lost in Serbia following the closure of Tanjug, the country's largest public broadcaster.

Far-right, anti-Islam group Pegida was also highlighted in the MMF report as a growing concern. German journalists have faced rising hostility when covering protests organised by the group. Reports submitted to the mapping project showed cases of assault and equipment being damaged.

In February, MMF project officer Hannah Machlin attended Unesco's conference in Paris entitled News Organisations Standing Up for the Safety of Journalists, where news editors and media leaders met to discuss best practice. Machlin, who was also there to talk about MMF, said: "One of the talks I attended at the conference was about the ongoing cases of impunity. During this meeting one of the panelists argued for tougher pressure on governments to create economic burdens on countries who are not punishing perpetrators for their crimes against journalists."

Index is now also part of the Council of Europe research project Journalists At Risk: Part of the Job? The project will launch a survey to gather qualitative and quantitative data about issues, including journalist safety and what leads to self-censorship.

Also in the past few months, Index's magazine editor Rachael Jolley spoke at the Swedish Library Association Libraries and Democracy conference about why libraries play an important role in giving people a conduit to knowledge, both online and in print.

And as part of Index's work to help musicians in exile, a special screening of They Will Have To Kill Us First, a documentary about persecuted musicians in Mali, was held at the Bulgari Hotel, London. The event helped raise money for Index's Music In Exile Fund, which was launched in October in partnership with Index and the film's producers, and will help a musician or group who are unable to play safely in their homeland.

Lastly, the Index on Censorship Freedom of Expression Awards will be announced

this year on 13 April at a gala evening at London's Unicorn Theatre. Female stand-up comedian Sakdiyah Ma'ruf, from Indonesia, and GreatFire, an organisation that tracks China's censorship, are among the nominees. More than 400 nominations were narrowed down to 20 for the 2016 shortlist, which celebrates the courage and creativity of those tackling censorship and fighting for freedom of expression around the world. The winners will also become part of Index's Awards Fellowship programme, which offers longer term, structured support. To shortlist the last 20 nominees, the first-ever, multi-location judges' breakfast was held. UK-based judges were able to join others online from Bahrain and Lagos – including former Index award

winner Nabeel Rajab, who is currently under a travel ban from the Bahraini authorities and unable to leave the country.

Ahead of the awards gala, last year's arts category winner, Moroccan rapper and human rights activist Mouad Belghouat, aka El Haqed, told Index what he'd gained from winning his award in 2015. He said: "Through Index, I met many great people from all over the world who share the same principles as me, and word of my case has spanned the breadth of the world." ⊗

Josie Timms is Index's editorial assistant and chair of the Index on Censorship youth advisory board. She is also the first Liverpool John Moores University/Tim Hetherington Fellow

ABOVE: Members of Index's youth board Madeleine Stone, Layli Foroudi, Simon Engelkes, Mariana Cunha e Melo and Emily Wright (left to-right clockwise) with posters saying why freedom of expression is important to them

T-shirted turmoil

END NOTE

45(01): 122/124 | DOI: 10.1177/0306422016643039

A few letters on cotton clothing shouldn't provoke fear within great state machines, but sometimes they do. **Vicky Baker** looks at why slogan shirts are more than a fashion statement

YELLOW T-SHIRTS ARE a legitimate national security concern, a court in Malaysia has ruled. The decision, related specifically to shirts with a Bersih 4 slogan, came in February after a group of citizens called for a review on the government's countrywide ban of the clothing. "The home minister has effectively 'criminalised' thousands of Malaysians who wore and still own the Bersih 4 T-shirt," said campaign leaders in a statement released shortly afterwards. "It is more than just a piece of cloth. The T-shirt represents our rights, freedom and expression."

Six months earlier, the street of Kuala Lumpur and other Malaysian cities turned yellow as they filled with protesters from Bersih 4 campaign, a nationwide protest movement for more transparent governance (Bersih meaning clean in Malay). Ahead of

a series of rallies, the home minister banned the shirts. Thousands of Malaysians defied him, and the press and social media spoke of a new-found xanthophobia, a fear of the colour yellow.

Activist Ivy Josiah, who attended the Bersih demonstration in Kuala Lumpur, said the fear initially ran both ways. She told Index that many participants turned up with their T-shirts hidden in their bags. "Once they realised no arrests were taking place, they quickly changed. Overwhelmingly, the vast majority of protesters wore the Bersih 4 T-shirts in defiance," she said. "The government got disturbed because a people's movement this large could upset the status quo."

In countries where people are unable to speak freely, letting your chest do the talking is a bold step. It shows how you stand by your opinions publically and resolutely. But it comes with risks.

Two years have now passed since Egyptian student Mahmoud Hussein was arrested in Cairo, aged 18, while walking home from a peaceful commemoration of the 2011 Tahrir Square uprising. It was the wording on his T-shirt that caught the authorities' attention: "Nation without torture". On the back was a picture of a police officer torturing a citizen.

Hussein was jailed immediately. He's been in prison ever since, despite not being formally charged with a crime. And he's been tortured himself. Last year Amnesty International reported alleged electric-shock treatment to his face, testicles, back and hands.

His brother, Tarek, told Index that the state has broken its own criminal code laws by overstepping the two-year maximum for pre-trial detention. "I do not know why Mahmoud is kept locked up all this period," he said. "The fear, in my opinion, is not from the T-shirt, but from the dream on the T-shirt: a nation without torture, a nation where nobody gets offended, a nation in which all sectors from different political ideologies and religions are respected."

Indonesian author Eliza Vitri Handayani staged her own T-shirt protest last year after her book launch was cancelled at Ubud Writers and Readers Festival in Bali. Festival organisers had come under pressure from local police to cancel a variety of events – mostly those related to the mass killings of communist civilians and party members in 1965-66 following an attempted coup, but,

It was the wording on his T-shirt that caught the authorities' attention ... Hussein was jailed immediately

as a police chief told CNN Indonesia, there were also concerns over sessions related to "ethnicity, religion and race".

Handayani didn't see her coming-of-age novel, From Now On Everything Will Be Different, as particularly subversive, but her event was among those struck off. Other authors in the same position responded by putting on their own fringe events in nearby cafes, but Handayani was worried she couldn't guarantee the safety of her guests and so came up with an alternative plan. She printed five T-shirts, each carrying a different, politically critical excerpt from the novel, and she wore a different one to the festival each day.

"I wanted to promote the book and also highlight what was going on, so I thought: maybe I can wear my work?" she told Index. "It created an excuse to talk to people. I sold all the copies I took with me and I also got interviewed by the press. I hope that coverage put pressure back on to the authorities to protect citizens' freedom of expression."

She said she'd do it again if she needed to. She has already fashioned a dress from her book proofs, which she wore to an event in Norway. "What women wear in Indonesia is already subject to a lot of restrictions. →

OPPOSITE: Malaysian protesters march wearing yellow T-shirts with the Bersih 4 slogan during a rally in Kuala Lumpur in August 2015. The shirts, which demonstrators wore while campaigning for more governmental transparency and Prime Minister Najib Razak's resignation, were banned by the state

ABOVE: Indonesian author Eliza Vitri Handayani wearing quotes from her novel on her T-shirt after her book launch was cancelled because of police concerns over its subject matter

→ Perhaps this a way to kill two birds with one stone?"

Footballers have also long been drawing attention to causes – from burning social issues to matters of their own egos – by lifting up their shirts to reveal a message to the crowds. The International Football Association Board formally banned statements on undershirts in 2014, ahead of the World Cup in Brazil. But this didn't stop Russian footballer Dmitri Tarasov making a show of

But can a provocative slogan transform into hate speech? This is an issue currently under debate in South Africa

support for President Putin during a match in Turkey in February. "Most polite president" were the words emblazoned on his front; tensions between the countries have been fraught since Turkey shot down a Russian jet last November.

But can a provocative slogan transform into hate speech? This is an issue currently under debate in South Africa. In February,

a black student at University of the Witwatersrand wore a plain, white T-shirt, on which he'd scrawled, "Being black is shit" on one side and "Fuck white people" on the other. He told South Africa's The Times, "I was feeling hatred because it was times of financial exclusion." The university condemned the shirt and the student is due to appear before the South African Human Rights Commission on charges of hate speech. Since then a University of Cape Town student has been photographed in another T-shirt bearing a hand-written inscription: "Kill All Whites."

Howard Besser, a professor of cinema studies at New York University in the USA, has been collecting slogan T-shirts since the 1980s. He estimates he has around 3,000 of them, 500 of which have been catalogued online (besser.tsoa.nyu.edu/T-Shirts/). Among recent additions is the "Hands up, don't shoot" shirt worn during the 2014 Black Lives Matter protests, which was sparked by an unarmed black teenager, Trayvon Martin, being shot dead by a neighbourhood watch coordinator.

"Unlike a leaflet or an ad on TV, someone cannot fully avoid seeing the slogan on a T-shirt," said Besser. "Slogans are quick, and if they're clever and/or surrounded by nice colours or graphics, they can be very effective. Year-round, I average about one person per day stopping me to discuss the topic on my T-shirt. With some shirts I'll get more than half a dozen people stopping me in a single day."

Whether the aim of a slogan T-shirt is to shock, amuse or inspire, they are designed to be talking points. That doesn't mean that all of them have something worthwhile to say. But for those that choose their clothing to display defiant, unspoken messages, the medium is as powerful as ever and no passing fashion will change that. ⊗

Vicky Baker is deputy editor of Index on Censorship magazine. She tweets @vickybaker